Journey to Whole Peace

Ericka —
you are truly a blessing to me in more ways than you know. I am thankful our paths crossed at this perfect time in our lives! God Bless You!

Cassie

JOURNEY to WHOLE PEACE

A woman's life journey of mistakes to ultimately discover God's love for her

CASSIE BOOTH

TATE PUBLISHING
AND ENTERPRISES, LLC

Journey to Whole Peace
Copyright © 2014 by Cassie Booth. All rights reserved.

No part of this publication may be reproduced, stored in a retrieval system or transmitted in any way by any means, electronic, mechanical, photocopy, recording or otherwise without the prior permission of the author except as provided by USA copyright law.

Scripture taken from the *Holy Bible, New International Version®*.

The opinions expressed by the author are not necessarily those of Tate Publishing, LLC.

Published by Tate Publishing & Enterprises, LLC
127 E. Trade Center Terrace | Mustang, Oklahoma 73064 USA
1.888.361.9473 | www.tatepublishing.com

Tate Publishing is committed to excellence in the publishing industry. The company reflects the philosophy established by the founders, based on Psalm 68:11,
"The Lord gave the word and great was the company of those who published it."

Book design copyright © 2014 by Tate Publishing, LLC. All rights reserved.
Cover design by *Jim Villaflores*
Interior design by *Caypeeline Casas*

Published in the United States of America
ISBN: 978-1-63185-501-6
Biography & Autobiography / Personal Memoirs
14.07.28

DEDICATION

I dedicate this book to my children: Brandon, Cayla, Cierra and Genevieve. It is my hope to show them the love of God in all of my actions. Before I knew God's love for me, I was not even close at getting it right. I am hopeful that my children will see that all the mistakes and experiences I made stemmed from not knowing the love of God and being consumed with pride. It is my prayer that they will see him in me now, and know the love that he has for them much sooner in their lives than I ever realized it. I now know what love is, and I live every day to express his love to others. My children are what matter most in this journey. The tradition of passing on of hurtful behavior, confusion, and identity crisis ends with me. It is very necessary that my children learn their identity in Christ and find and fulfill his purpose—to be able to live life as it is intended for them to be lived, to the fullest. I praise God that all the hurts of my past were not wasted, and he has used every tear I shed to wash me clean as snow with his free gift of love.

In loving memory of my Grandpa Jones

My Grandpa William Jones, Deacon in the Catholic Church

ACKNOWLEDGEMENTS

I would like to acknowlege the people that have stuck by my side during the unfolding of this amazing journey. People are put in our lives for a reason, a season, or a lifetime. Throughout my life, up until this time, I have had trouble recognizong which category to put people in. At the completeion of this book, I can give acknowledgement to two people that really understand me on many different levels. These are people who pour into me as much as I have poured into them. These women have all come across my path first as consistent, successful clients, but I now realize these women were strategically placed in my life for a reason. These women are my lifetime friends and sisters in Christ. They are Heather McAdams, and Amy Grothoff. There are no words to let these women know how thankful I am for all their support and love in all the seasons of my life.

Special thanks to Pastors David and Nicole Crank of Faith Church. I spent time with them on a mission trip in October of 2013. My calling was taken to a different level after that trip. I learned what leadership was all about through their hands on approach of helping others. I was able to learn how to act at the level of my calling I learned the importance of being the best I can be to go back and be a blessing to others. Thank you for your love and leadership, I will never be the same!

Cassie and Pastors David And Nicole Crank
Mission Trip, Beach Baptism,
West Palm Beach Florida Oct.2013

CONTENTS

Foreword 11

PART 1 To Whom Do I Belong;
          and Where Am I Going ? 13

Who Am I? 15
Who Do They Think I Am? 19
What Was My Parents´ Motivation? 23
Who Will Love Me? 31
Could This Be Love? 43
Another Chance at Love? 53
Is This Who I Am? 63
Will This Cycle Ever End? 71
How Can I Find Peace? 81
God, Is That You? 91

PART 2 "You Are My Child.
          I Will Make a Way for You" 109

God Is with Me 111
God Is in Control 119
Reshaping and Molding Begins 127
Make My Path Straight, Lord 133
My Peace I Give to You 139
I Trust You, Lord 147

God Really Is Love 151
Train Me up to Do Your Will 163
A Glimpse of His Plan Revealed to Me 193

Afterword 209
Testimonials 213

FOREWORD

This being the day after signing the contract to write this book with Tate Publishing, I stand in awe and amazement at how great our God truly is. My prayer at the start of 2013 was simply, "God, show me my special talents and use me to do your will."

On January 15th, I began Whole Peace Fitness. God dropped the business name and logo on my heart, and then he sent all right clients. In one month, my clientele tripled in size. They were seeing results, and their lives were being changed. God gave me the strength to run the race that he clearly set before me.

Not sure of what would come next but wanting to do a full-time fitness ministry, I started trying to do things in my own will. I was focused on corporate wellness and trying to get contracted agreements to get myself out of my job in municipal government. I am sure God was just laughing at my efforts, as he had other plans for me that I was unaware of at the time.

Continuing in my prayer life to always be thankful for what has already been done, and asking for guidance on what was to come next, I was blown away about what did come next.

It was put on my heart to write my story. As I have heard a great teacher of the gospel say, "When God puts something on you to do, you do it, or you feel like you will die if you don't." That was exactly the kind of conviction I received. I had no clue about how to go about it. I have always kept a journal of all my thoughts, and I love writing notes. I started looking on the Internet, and Tate just literally popped up on my screen. I e-mailed to Alana Duffle my ideas; she told me I needed a manuscript to submit. I was not sure how to do that or what it would entail. God equipped me to do everything. Palm Sunday of 2013 we got a massive snowstorm in our area. I sat down at the computer with this heavy urge to write. I started, and the words just flowed out. The power of the Holy Spirit was working within me. I just went with it. Before I knew it, I had been writing for hours. I got bold and attached my manuscript to Alana. I literally had my eyes closed, and I was holding my breath when I hit send. That same day, Palm Sunday, I got a response from Alana (that was not auto-generated). She said I would be hearing from her soon. I was in shock.

My prayers were then, "Lord, if this is your will, I know you will make a way for me." Later that week, I received word that Tate loved my work, and they then offered me a contract. God's will, indeed. I was not thinking about writing a book; I knew nothing about the process. It was *his* will; he equipped me to do it.

The week prior to my signing that contract, I was attacked by all of the forces of darkness. I was not shaken; I am aware of the spiritual battle that is very real. I also knew that battle had already been won, and I stand on the promises that the Lord gives to his children. He has started a good work in me, and he will see it through to completion.

PART 1

*To Whom Do I Belong;
and Where Am I Going ?*

WHO AM I?

Most of my life, up until a couple of years ago, I had no understanding of who I was or what love really was. Like most young girls, I equated love with sex. What I have just recently come to realize is that God is love. What this means is if one does not know God, he cannot truly know what love is. Without God, we just have our own incomplete and distorted interpretation of what it is by what we feel, and how it was shown to us through various people in our lives. True love is only known through having a real relationship with our Creator. That is a revelation that was put on my heart during the process of writing my story. During this process, I was asked directly by my mother and my dad if I ever felt loved by them. My honest heartfelt answer was no. It is my hope to show through this book why my answer was no at that time I do realize their efforts as parents were centered around the fact that they loved me, but along the way, that did not get transferred to me. I know they cared for me, and there is no doubt they sacrificed for me. I know now that if they knew the true love of God, their efforts may have landed and would have had a greater affect on me in a more positive way. My story right from the start is about my looking for love, significance, value, and worth—those which only can come from God, for all of us.

We were a middle-income black family living above our means. It was my younger brother and me. We had the same mother but different fathers. I came from what appeared to be a stable home. I know now that my parents did the best they could with what they knew. My dad who raised me was an ordained minister and a mechanic, and my mother was a nurse that worked nights. My mother got pregnant with me when she was ninteen years old, and my biological father denied me as his ever since my mother told him she was pregnant. My mother tells me when she became pregnant, she thought about not having me at times. She had it set in her mind when a girl she played softball with, Casondra, talked her out of seeking an abortion. Mom ended up naming me after the girl that convinced her to have me.

My biological father's parents, mostly my grandpa, always accepted me, so that created a strange dynamic from the start. My grandma mostly sided with her son, my father, but tried to go along for the sake of her husband. She did do things with me when grandpa was not around. She would show me how to crochet plant holders, and we would make latch hook rugs. I could tell she was trying with me because she had such a love for her husband. I do think that since I was such an awesome kid, I may have been growing on her a little bit too. There were definitely times I could feel her animosity toward me. From what I heard about my father by various family members, he loved to drag race cars and drank a lot when he was younger. Also, from what I have heard, he grew up to be an alcoholic who never married and had no other kids. The only time I have ever seen him was at my grandpa's funeral years later; he was drinking at the wake and even tried to hit on me, as he did not even know I was his daughter.

Since my paternal grandparents were there for me, and not so much my brother, that created some rifts in our family. Nothing was ever fully explained to me as to why I had these grandparents and my brother didn't. I think my mother carried some shame associated with the situation; therefore, it was really hard for her to fully explain everything to me clearly.

There was also tension between my mother and my dad regarding the matter. Dad was the only father I had known since age two; he adopted me and gave me his name. He did not think it was important for me to have any ties with my paternal grandparents. To him, even to this day, he felt it was disrespectful to even give mention that I was not biologically his child.

There were good times I remember with all of us together—Mom, Dad, my brother, and I. We would spend Friday nights having pizza, and we would watch *The Dukes of Hazzard* and *The Incredible Hulk*. On some Saturdays, we would drive to the city and get the best Chinese food. My brother and I usually could not wait until we got all the way home to eat the egg rolls, and they were always so hot that we would bring clean socks. We would put the egg roll in the sock and hang it out the window to cool, so we could eat them on the ride home.

Dad worked as a head mechanic at a gas station in Rock Hill. Every week, when he got paid in the summer time, we would all go to his job and have fried chicken and strawberry soda on his lunch break. There was a picnic table that was off to the side of the parking lot there where he worked. After we'd eat lunch, Dad would go back to work. Mom would pull the car up to the pump, and the pump attendants would run out and wash the windshield and fill up the car and have her sign a pink ticket. This ticket would be the amount they would take off Dad's paycheck. Sometimes, my brother and I would get to run inside and put candy, chips, or soda on the pink ticket too. We always felt like royalty when we pulled up. I wish I could say that the good times I had with my family made more of an impression on how I lived my life as an adult more than the strange occurrences did.

My grandfather was the kindest man I ever knew. He took me everywhere with him. He was an important man in the city of Kirkwood. He did a lot of social work in a poor area called Meacham Park. He believed in God and knew God's love, and it showed in how he treated everyone. It was like he had this light about him, which attracted people.

He smoked a pipe sometimes, and he always had peppermint candy on hand. He had the best laugh ever. He'd let me sit in his lap all the time, and I loved the way he smelled. He was at every dance recital or show or play I was ever in, with his camera in hand. He had a prison ministry. He would go to prisons and talk to young men and boys about the love God had for them. He gave them small pocket Bibles, clean underclothing, soap, and razors. He was hope for these young men and boys. He showed them love. I remember going with him once to the juvenile detention center. He brought me to the recreation room area, and I got to see how some of the teens he worked with responded to him. It was awesome; they would light up when he walked in the room. They'd run right over. "How ya doing, Mr. Jones?" they'd say. I'd beam with pride because that was my grandpa. He had retired from the post office and wore a big shiny watch they gave him for his many years of service. Everywhere we went, everyone always knew him, and I was proud to be his granddaughter. He would take me fishing and to the horse races. I really felt his love for me. When we were together, nothing else mattered. Looking back now, I see that love my grandfather had for was real and very healthy, and he shared that same love for all people. Unfortunately for me, during that time, there was so much controversy surrounding that love. In my family, I never really saw just how important that was for me.

This was a spiritual battle from the start, I never realized until now. The forces of darkness, which are very real, were keeping me from the light in my grandpa, even at a very young age. My family had seeds of shame, guilt, pride, and jealousy rooted around this relationship I had with my grandfather. All these things were just strongholds for the enemy to use to deceive and destroy that pure love I was shown.

WHO DO THEY THINK I AM?

My life at home was much segmented. We were active members of the church. My dad was an ordained minister, but we did not go to the church he went to since it was an all-black church with no kids' activities. My mother brought us up in an all-white Baptist church in Ballwin. She wanted us to have kids' activities and a Bible study for her. She always made sure we had the best of everything. We had name brand clothing and tennis shoes. Mom has always kept her hair long, and so my hair was always pressed and kept long and perfect. I remember her making me wear a scarf on my head in the winter, instead of a hat in order to keep my hair just right. I remember when I got baptized; my mother seemed to be more concerned with what my hair would look like after the ceremony than anything else involving what it actually meant to be baptized.

Giving our children the best has nothing to do with material or worldly things. Showing them the love of God and all he is will always better equip them for anything they may face. Putting on the full armor of God is better than any named branded clothing.

Growing up, we lived in the suburbs of West County, the best part of town. We were a lower middle-income black family, living out of our means to make that happen. There were not many black families in this area in the early 1980s. There were kids from the inner city that were bussed in to go to the schools we were privileged to attend. My mother hated that. She never wanted us hanging out with the "city niggas," as she would call them. She felt like she worked hard for us to afford to live where there were nice schools to get away from the city environment—and here they were, the people she was trying to get us away from, going to our schools for free. It is so ironic that my grandpa was the one showing people less fortunate unconditional love all the time. He went straight to the degenerates of society and showed them love and hope. Mom was showing us to run the opposite direction and never become like "them." When she was younger, in the 50s, the black kids were mean to her and put her down because she was poor. I really think that in her head she felt she could really prove something if she could be more like the white kids.

My brother and I were very different from most kids we knew. We were often told by the other white kids that we didn't "act black." We were told by the black kids that we "acted white." I think the black kids really did not accept us as much as the white kids did. I can remember being taunted and teased by black girls who were from the city. I was always scared whenever a group of black kids were around. I could hear them say, "She really thinks she's white," and they would laugh and mock me. I would always walk out of the way to get to my classes if there were a group of them together. I would always worry about getting beat up because I did not know how to fight or defend myself if I ever needed to. It made it harder because the black boys who were bussed in seemed to take a liking to me, and that really made the city girls out to get me. I now know that seed of fear was planted in me. *We are not given a spirit of fear.*

I remember one time when my Auntie Kathryn had a job at a fast food place, there was this girl who worked with her that would talk about a girl at her school that was a cheerleader that only hung out with white people and talked and acted white. The more she would describe me and talk about me to my aunt and everyone who worked there. My aunt figured out she was talking about me. My aunt said a few words and set that girl straight.

I really only had about two good friends who were black; all my friends were white. I fit right in with them. Those two friends were "county brownies," just like me. They lived in the county. That just furthered my identity crisis, I do believe. I started "acting black" around the blacks and "acting white" around the whites. They seemed to do the same as I did. I acted "churched" around my church friends, and did whatever to fit in around the "un-churched "kids. I had no idea who I was, but I was one good actor faking my way through.

It seemed even our extended family members even ostracized us. My Aunt Kathryn, who is my mother's youngest sister and very close to my age, would try to teach me how to fight and dance and fit in with the black kids. She could not believe how "white" I was. She was always trying to help me fit in. Can you believe I had to be shown how to fit in? Our mother would limit our time around our family. They laughed because I could not dance like them. I was told I had no rhythm and that I talked white. This had to be very troublesome for me as a youth, perhaps it was the reason I wet the bed until I was close to twelve years old. Did my mother not realize that something was bothering me, that I could not express to her? That was a very hurtful thing, being outcast by my own family. Who am I, and who would show me the love I so desperately needed?

WHAT WAS MY PARENTS' MOTIVATION?

We really had nothing at all to do with my dad's side of the family. My dad's family was very strange. He was married before he met my mother, and he had a daughter. He would always call her my sister. She was really my brother's sister, since they shared the same biological father. I did not feel any connection to her. My dad tried to force that, but it never really happened between us. My mother was very much against that also. My dad's family was always getting evicted and moving from house to house. There were about ten people always living in the one house. His mom was heavyset and needed dentures but would never wear them, her hair was always a mess, and she always had house shoes on. Whenever we were around her, she would always have food sitting out. Her words were always, "Go ahead and get yourself a plate." She was always trying to feed us. She was a very loving, funny woman. My dad's brothers and sisters were crazy about my younger brother, but they treated me a little different since I was another man's daughter. Mom did not want me to spend the night or anything; she feared me being molested like she was. My mom was always amazed at how their family could always find somewhere to live so fast. They would get pretty nice houses in not so bad areas in the county. Mom and dad would argue constantly about us going around those uncivilized people. She always told us she would not have us around a bunch of "niggas." How confusing is that? Our family thought that we were stuck up and that we thought we were too good for them. I can see how they would think that, but for me, it was far from the truth. I wanted to have a connection with them and understand where I came from. My mother had it in her head that she was going to do everything in her power to raise her children right, and that meant giving us the best. During all this, I never really felt loved for who I was. I felt like I was being dressed up to be something she wanted me to be. This was something she never had for herself. I do not blame her because all she knew was that she was going to do better for her kids than what was done for her.

Mom grew up the oldest of nine kids. Her mother was always working to provide for her kids, and there really was no father figure there for the kids. Her brothers and sisters mostly had all different fathers, and that was sort of a mystery to them from what I recall. Her mother—my grandma—was a godly woman also, but her lifestyle did not exactly reflect that. When Mom was pregnant with me, her mother had just had her ninth child, my Aunty Kathryn. Mom would tell me how the black kids would make fun of her and were mean because she was so poor and she had ragged clothes. She learned how to fight so she could defend her younger brothers and sisters in school. She told me she lied about getting Christmas presents to a girl at school. She told the girl she got Russian boots and a mohair sweater. The girl kept saying she was going to come to her house to see the gifts, since Mom never wore them to school. Even back then, she needed to be something she was not, to prove herself. My mother spent a lot of time with her grandmother, whom she loved very much. She lived with her for a while. She showed my mother a genuine love. Her grandmother worked nights, leaving my mom alone with her grandfather. My mother was sexually abused by her grandfather from the age of nine until age twelve. She loved her grandmother so much that she could never bring herself to tell her. Hearing my mother tell me that she loved her grandmother showed me that what she thought was love was not demonstrated to her as God's love. She tells me that she did not tell her grandmother of the abuse, but I think that her view of love was wrong just in making that statement. She loved her grandmother, but held back from her I think because she was afraid of how her grandmother would view her, or perhaps afraid she would hurt her grandmother. But that is not what true love is, as God has intended. Perfect love casts out fear.

She was never able to fully heal from the scars of her past before I came along; this was evident in the way she raised me. She had me, and I became the object of her affection and also a distraction to her pain. Within two years, she was in love again, and married my dad. That is how it goes in life. We all have scars, and we look for something else to cover and heal them.

Anything other than the blood of Jesus just will not do it. Things in life will only distract us from the pain temporarily, but if we do not lay our burdens down so we can be fully healed, we will carry those burdens right into hurtful behavior toward those we interact with.

I am very thankful that I can look back and recognize why things were the way they were, and how they affected me in my adult life.

When Mother met my dad, I was two years old. He was on leave from the army, and his aunt lived next door to mom's house in Webster. He saw a picture of my mom on his aunt's mantel and had to meet her. He tells the story that he fell in love with me, and carried me around everywhere, so he just had to marry my mother. They got married in 1972, and my brother was born in 1974.

Dad was an auto mechanic who smoked cigarettes even after he'd promise us every week he would quit. He cussed and told dirty jokes when it was not Sunday. He'd listen to old Richard Pryor records at night when he thought we were asleep. I can remember the filthy language emanating throughout the house, and he would just laugh and laugh. He did not drink alcohol. Since he was an auto mechanic, he was always greasy and grimy; Mom would always stay on him about getting cleaned up. The only day he ever looked presentable was on Sundays. Remember, he was an ordained minister at a black church that my mother, brother, and I did not attend. Needless to say, his walk with the Lord was a little questionable. He was a very good provider, but he was not around for any of our activities because he was always at work. He is a funny man who has a lot of friends, and he would do anything to help anyone out. He and my mother insisted on having the best for their kids. Dad would work all kinds of side jobs to try to make ends meet. He would work late, come home, and fall asleep on the couch in his work clothes. Mom hated that.

Anytime I needed money for lunch, picture day, a dance, or whatever, I would leave a note on the fridge, and the money I needed would be there the next day. Dad always had cash on hand. I could always depend on him for money. Emotionally, I was detached from my dad. We did not talk much since he was never around. Looking back, he pretty much did whatever he could for me, and I knew I could always count on him to provide in a material sense. Was that love to me? No, not really. Dad showed his love by provding for the family. What I needed at that time was his time and attention. Mom was more of the disciplinarian of the household. Dad was there to provide her with reinforcements. She definitely dominated the relationship, and the household. She paid all of the bills. She managed the money Dad would make. She did not like the fact that Dad would walk around with money in his pockets, and she would have to get it from him to pay all the bills. Since that is not the way God intended for a married woman to function in a marriage that would ultimately lead to its demise.

I do know that Dad felt his importance to the family was to provide. Dad worked hard on cars all the time, in hot or cold weather. He showed his love for the family by sacrificing his time with making money. The money he made was used to help us live above our means, to try to be something we were not, which by his being gone all the time, I was emotionally detached from him; and it would upset him when I went to spend time with my biological grandpa. How did this show me love?

I remember Dad getting a swing set to go in the backyard of our house. It was a big deal to have one, and all the other houses had one in the backyard. Dad went out and bought it, and then brought in the basement to put it all together. He worked on it all day. Then it dawned on him, since he put it together in the basement—how would he get it in the backyard now that it was all put together? He was cussing up a storm once he realized he'd have to do the entire thing over. He did, but he never did get the slide on. He was so tired and stressed with the entire project that he just stopped and never did get around to putting the slide on. The slide was the most important part to us kids, and he never did get around to putting it on; his lack of time with us led to a lot of broken promises.

Mom had us in all kinds of extracurricular activities—dance classes, gymnastics, and piano lessons. I was always in some kind of choir concert, dance contest, recital, or some other kind of performance. My brother played little league football and soccer, I was a cheerleader. All these activities were costly. She worked so hard to keep up with the white people. I learned early on a double-minded way of thinking and acting. I was a certain way with my youth group and church friends, and then fitting in with the cool kids at school. I was a certain way with the white kids, and yet an entirely different way with the black kids. I was a bedwetter up until I was almost twelve. Wouldn't that cause concern in a parent? All these years, I looked at it as just something else I did, but in writing this book, I realize it was glaringly evident that something was wrong. I was having some sort of internal struggle, which was indeed the case. My mother only intended the best for her kids; however, my perception of it was all true of my reality.

I took dance at a small studio in Des Peres. Mom and I found it one day when were we driving back from somewhere. The owner was in the window, painting a sign in for this new studio. We stopped in and asked about classes. We were tired of the studio I was currently in and were also looking for a shorter drive. The dance teacher said she had a studio in House Springs and that this new studio would be her new second location. The classes were exactly what we were looking for, so Mom signed me up. This dance teacher was amazing. She took a liking to me right away. She had a daughter a few years older than me, and we became good friends. There was another girl who came from the studio where I was before, and so we were all in the same class.

Before long, it was like I was the new adopted kid in their white family. We were always doing recitals, contests, and even demonstrations at the local department stores. I remember long car rides with these girls, as we would go back and forth from the two studios. We would laugh and play silly games with people in the cars around us. We'd make fun of the toothless help in the country diners we would stop in to eat from time to time, after a long day of dance. My mom would let me just go wherever they needed me to go. My lessons ended up being free before long, since I was taking extra classes and helping out with the younger kid's classes. My friend and her mother did not always get along, and a lot of times it would cause problems since her mother would pay so much attention to me. Once again, I was being shown love, but it was surrounded with confusion and disappointment. It was yet another strange dynamic. She would often get angry and talk back and cuss her mother out. I just could not believe it. I thought her mother was wonderful and did not deserve to be treated like that. I did not understand how she could treat her mother like that. I would tell my friend how I felt about it. She would just tell me that I just did not understand. All I knew was that her mother was someone who believed in me and showed me love, yet she had a hard time expressing that to her own daughter. I did have encouraging adult people all around me showing me love. Looking back now, I can really appreciate that.

I also remember taking piano lessons. Mom wanted me to play and they even got a piano so I could practice. The lessons were expensive, I remembered my dad complaining about the cost. I had to take theory class also I remember hating to practice everyday and I also remember not being very good. My mother wanted me to be good but music was not my gift, at all. The one thing that sticks out most about piano lesson was my teacher, Sister Alice. She was a catholic nun and she was so sweet and patient with me. She could tell I did not like playing the piano but she was so loving and sweet. I remember how she would correct the placement of my fingers and instruct me to keep my hands soft. she would give me a lemon drop after every lesson. This was once again some one who knew God's love and was expressing it to me.

WHO WILL LOVE ME?

As a teen I was popular, but very promiscuous. I starting having sex and acting out at age fifteen, and to think I just stopped wetting the bed three years prior. I would sneak out of the house and go to parties. Dad was a hard sleeper who snored very loud; Mom worked nights, so she was gone for work on some weekends. It was easy to sneak out, or even to sneak boys in. I drank alcohol, smoked pot, and cigarettes. I even tried speed at one time. Even through all my inner turmoil, I would always take time to journal my thoughts and spend quiet time in my room. I was searching for something to fill the void within me.

A person can have the best of all things, but if they do not know the true love, which is the love of Christ, they really have nothing.

I was a freshman in high school, dating a senior who was very popular—the senior class president, and prom king. I was on the pom pon squad, so by now, I thought I was all that. I went to the senior prom as a freshman, and I was on the prom court at age fifteen. My mom was so proud of me. Why would that make her proud of me? I did not do anything but get a popular guy to want me.

During my freshman year, my friends started calling me Cassie, and my mother really did not like that. She would let everyone know that she had named me "Casondra," and that was what she wanted me to be called. Yes, what she wanted me to be called. She hated it when people would mispronounce my name, they would call me "Cassandra." The *o* in my name is actually a long *o*, and no one ever got it right. I was fine with being called Cassie.

Toward the end of my freshman year, it was my boyfriend's senior night graduation party lock-in. He left the party early somehow to come and see me. He was the class president, so I guess he was able to leave. He snuck into my room just to be with me. We were just lying in my bed. It was really late at night, and for some reason, my brother came in my room and saw him in bed with me. My brother freaked out and ran to get my dad. I told my boyfriend to hide in the closet. My dad found him in the closet—then he went nuts. My boyfriend left the house and Dad went off on me. Dad was pacing the floor, looking for a cigarette, not sure what to do or say. It was almost like he was overreacting, like he was going to have a nervous breakdown or something. Since Mom worked nights, she did not hear about this until the next day. I remember my dad telling Mom to go and have me checked out to make sure I was not pregnant. I assured them we were not having sex—yes, I told a huge lie. That would have been the perfect opportunity for her to open her eyes and see that her daughter needed her. I think for appearances' sake, Mom never did take me to get checked out; I was only grounded and could not go anywhere for a while, which was bad timing since the school year ended, and my boyfriend would be going off to college far away, and I would be devastated.

When my boyfriend did go away to college, we tried to make it work. I would get in so much trouble for the long distance phone calls. I was calling him two to three times a day. My parents would get so furious when the phone bill came. Eventually, he broke it off with me, and I was so devastated. I felt like I was nothing without him. After all, he was who I was, right? Not long after he broke it off with me, I started sleeping with all of his friends who were in town going to the community college, or ones who were a year younger than he was and still in high school. It was horrible. I am not sure if I was trying to get back at him for leaving me, or maybe I was trying to replace what I thought I had with him. I remember going through this cycle of just having random sex. I just wanted someone, anyone to love me.

I once told my mom I would be riding the late bus home from school, but instead I got on the regular bus and went to this field to meet a white boy and have sex with him on a rock. Yes, a rock—a huge boulder in the middle of the woods near our house. He did not want to be my boyfriend of course; he just wanted the inner, most sacred part of me, and I just gave it to him. I remember walking home after that carrying such shame in that. It was like I had no control in what I was doing, like I was outside myself, watching my body do all these things that I did not want to be doing.

> I do not understand what I do. For what I want to do I do not do, but what I hate I do.
>
> Romans 7:15 (NIV)

By this time, my parents bought a new house, so we moved. I had to change high schools in my junior year. I went from Parkway school district to Rockwood school district. This was a good thing for me since I was starting to develop a bad reputation. I got the chance to make new friends and try to start over again. I made the cheerleading squad. It was a coed squad, and I was the only black girl on the squad, so that was an honor for me, and my mother. From that moment, I was labeled the cute black girl on the squad. Since I could do gymnastics, and I only weighed 105 pounds, I went up in a lot of the stunts. I really stood out. My mother was so proud of me.

I had an awesome gymnastics coach who would really take a great interest in all of her gymnasts. She was an amazing lady. I used to always use bad language whenever I would mess up or fall off the balance beam. My coach was constantly telling me how important it was for me to watch my mouth. I also had this bad habit of saying "I'm sorry" all the time. I would say it in regard to everything. She would tell me to stop being sorry; there was no reason for me to be sorry, just to correct the mistake and move on. She was right about that, not sure I truly grasped that back then. I just remained sorry for a long time. I also remember always asking people if they were mad at me. It was like I had this hidden bad conscience of always feeling sorry and worried about people being mad at me. The coach helped me to see then the words that came out of my mouth were extremely important. She was really right. Thank you, Coach Granna.

Before long at my new school, I was dating another star athlete who was again older than me, and then I dated another athlete who was younger than me. In fact, most of the teachers in school did know me since I dated the popular athletes. It was like I had some sort of notoriety in that. If I were late to class, they would let me slide. I remember being asked to go across the street to pick up lunch for a faculty member. I was given a hall pass to be late for class. Being a cheerleader, we had certain expectations. We could not be seen near the smoking lounge at school (Yes, we had a smoker's lounge for the kids at our high school. It was a marked-off area outside in the courtyard.)

Dad had gotten a brown Ford Pinto for my first car when I started driving. My birthday is in October, so I was younger than most of my classmates. I started driving much after a lot of them. Dad had paid cash for the car, and he was so proud. It had a bad transmission and would stick in reverse a few seconds before the car would actually back up. I did not care what kind of car I had; I was just happy to be able to drive. I was a varsity cheerleader, and I had girlfriends at the time who were sophomore cheerleaders and on the gymnastics team with me. They could not drive yet, so I would pick them up in my little brown pinto. These girls lived in much nicer subdivisions than I did. I would pull up in the mornings and honk my horn, and they would come right on out. These were white girls who were not stuck up in any way; they loved hanging out with me, and it was cool then to drive to school instead of riding the bus.

Mom made sure I did not drive on the highway, so everywhere I went I had to take main streets. I remember getting a job at the Galleria Mall and having to drive the entire way down Manchester road from our home in Ballwin. That route has to have at least thirty stoplights or more. She also forbade me to make turns going against the traffic. So then of course, it was way out of the question for me to ever drive to the city for any reason.

These were more seeds of fear that were planted. We are not given a spirit of fear, but one of love, power, and self-control. I had none of these things because I did not identify myself as a child of God. I had no identity.

Cheerleaders and athletes were considered ambassadors of the school. Our cheerleading squad had special notoriety with all the other schools also, since we went to the national championships in Florida, and at that time, we were the only high school that had a coed cheerleading squad. We were expected to behave a certain way whenever we had our cheer uniform on, or even our school jacket on. So, as you can imagine, most of us were a certain way in uniform. But out of uniform, it was a different story. We'd smoke cigarettes and drink wine coolers at the parties, just like all the other kids. I hung out with the in-crowd. I went to all the great parties. The kids I hung out with had money and really nice cars, and when their parents went out of town, they would have crazy parties at these extravagant homes. I got along with all the right kids, but I still was so lost as to who I was as an individual.

Among many high school friends, I had a really good friend named Stacey. She was a gorgeous white girl with really long, beautiful hair, and an even more beautiful smile. She laughed a lot, and I really liked hanging out with her. She had a Ford Mustang GT convertible that her daddy bought her. It was the prettiest shade of blue I had ever seen, and that car was the envy of everyone. The guys at school really thought it was cool. I remember we were driving around one day, and she needed to stop by her house for something. I remember her stopping by McDonald's to use the pay phone to call her mother to see if her dad was home since I was with her. I did not understand why she needed to know if her dad was home. She said her dad was home, so we could not go to her house. She said her dad did not like black people, and I could not go to the house when he was home. She was crying when she told me this. She said to me he does not understand that you really are not black, she had explained to me her mother had tried to tell her dad that I was different. *What?* I had been to her house plenty of times and had met her mother. Her father traveled a lot, so I had never met him. That moment was a real shocker. What was she saying? Who was I really? Why would anyone not allow me in their home? This added to the confusion and ongoing identity crisis.

    I had another good friend in high school I hung out with. She was a lot of fun. This girl was white, but she knew every rap song ever played. It was really amusing to hang with someone who liked "black music," so to speak. She had the new Ford Escort GT back then, It was a great car, so we'd hang out, and she'd play the loud beats, and we would laugh and have a great time. I liked all kinds of music back then, but listened to mostly pop and rock. She kept me up to date with all the rap and hip-hop stuff. I went with this friend to visit her dad one time. Her parents were divorced, and her dad remarried. Well, this was weird to me. Her father who was white was married to a black woman. That was something I sort of marveled at. I had slept with white boys, but never a girlfriend to one at that time, and here her father was married to a black woman. I am not sure why, but that was really neat to me.

    When I was a junior in high school, I got it in my head that I wanted to get my hair cut. Since I could drive myself, I made an appointment. We had a hairdresser whom mom and I went to every two weeks to get our hair done for as long as I could remember. I went to the hair dresser myself this time. I had a picture of Halle Berry and Toni Braxton with short hairstyles I liked. I was determined to cut my shoulder-length hair off. I did just that, and I felt amazing. I loved having my hair short. My mother had a fit about it, but I did not care because I loved it. She had worked so hard to take good care of my hair so it would grow long like hers. She equated long hair to being beautiful. To me, hair was just hair; I liked different hairstyles and trying different looks to change things up. Beauty comes from the inside. I am not sure she quite understood that. In a way, I felt relieved that I did not have to have my hair a certain way to be accepted.

At that time, I had a younger boyfriend I really loved, and we talked and shared everything together. We had been dating for at least eight months, which, for teenage romance, is a long time. I was a cheerleader, and he was a football player. He was a sophomore on the varsity team. In the spring, he played baseball, on the varsity team as well. One night, I got so mad because he had a baseball tournament and needed to rest up for a game, he decided not to go out that night with me. He was very serious about his sports. He was an American legion baseball player. That was a big deal back then. I went out that night anyway and had sex with a guy from the other team. I slept with the rival star athlete from the other school. If that wasn't enough, I went and told my boyfriend about it. I deliberately hurt him because of my own selfishness. I was getting more out of control with all of this identity crisis and confusion, and I was not even eighteen years old yet.

Mom had us in church and various activities that she wanted us to be in, but I never really felt loved. I always felt like Mom was trying to make me be everything she was not, and in that I felt like she never loved me for me just being me. I found the love I was looking for in boys. Promiscuity was a way I equated being wanted and loved. I equated love with sex. I was always in one relationship after another. It was always the popular athlete in school. I was trying to find my identity in them. In high school (ninth to twelfth grade) alone, I slept with over a dozen different boys. Back then, I did not really understand what was wrong with me. In writing this book, thinking back and counting the actual number of different boys I gave myself away to, I am so saddened at the realization that all I wanted was to be loved and accepted.

When it came to my senior year in 1988, my parents finally divorced. It really affected me in a lot of ways. I remember being humiliated on senior night for the cheerleaders and basketball players. We were to be escorted by our parents and announced to the crowd since we were seniors, and it was our last home game. My parents did not show up. I was bawling and completely humiliated. Everyone else's parents were there but mine. I was escorted out with my cheerleading sponsor with tears in my eyes—the only black cheerleader there with no parents. Apparently, my parents got into a fight over what time they were supposed to be there. My dad was going to be nice and pick mom up so they could attend together, but he was late and they missed the entire thing. All this effort they put into wanting us kids to have the best and working so hard and sacrificing things for us, only to end up just letting me down. I felt like I was built up so high just to be dropped to the ground.

When it came time to think about going to college, I just knew since Mom and Dad divorced there was no hope of me going away. Mom, my brother, and I were now living in a two-bedroom apartment. I was now sharing a room with my mother. There were plenty of other places we could have lived, and I could have had my own room, but mom insisted on being in the most affluent part of town, living above our means. My grandpa had a scholarship lined up for me through one of the many organizations he belonged to. It was a full scholarship to go the University of Tennessee. I would only need to cover room and boarding expenses. I was so thrilled at the opportunity to get away from my life and have a chance to start again. My grades were never the best—that is one thing Mom never really stressed upon us. I always got Cs and Bs. Math was extremely hard for me, so I struggled to get Ds. It seemed Mom was more concerned about the way we looked and the way we carried ourselves than focusing on our grades. It was as if she was grooming me to be a good wife, and neglected to teach me to have any confidence in myself to make it on my own, or to really get to know who I was as a person, to be independent. That may not have been what she intended, but my perception was defiantly my reality.

I know now that my parents failed me in showing me my identity in Christ. I was not told and did not see demonstrated what God says about me. I had no idea I was made for a purpose, that he had plans for my future and me. I was not shown that I was special in *his* sight. I should have been shown that it did not matter what I talked like or looked like, and that I should learn to look at people's hearts and not their skin color. I would have known the Father's love and comfort and would not have needed to search for it in the arms of one man after another.

Where my special talents nurtured? What were my special gifts? In all the activities I was put in, what did I stand out mostly in? Looking back now, I would have to say being in front of people putting on a show, making them clap for me. I am really good, but don't look too closely and what I am carrying inside me."

My mother did not know the true love of God for herself, so she could not have possibly passed it on to me. My mother was so wrapped up in how the world viewed me, and redeeming herself through me, that she forgot that she missed the most important thing. Yes, she got us to church and did all the right things, but somehow she missed the mark. It is so simple, many do miss it. The world is full of Satan's distractions that people get away from what is really important. The focus many times is on comparing ourselves to others around us—to try to be better or special, without knowing we are special in God's eyes just the way we are.

When we are wrapped up in the world view, we miss out on all the goodness God has for us.

Since the college in Tennessee was a primarily black college and so far away, Mom refused the college scholarship for me. She was completely opposed to it, and so it was that simple. I did not go, that was the end of that. I was really hurt, what she did at that very moment was plant a huge seed of self-doubt within me, along with more confusion in me by saying I would never make it there with all those black people. I wanted to just scream, *Mom, I am black! We are black!* I did enroll at the community college in Kirkwood, and I did pretty well with the classes I took, even though I did not really know what I wanted to study. I was just taking general classes to get an idea of what it was I wanted to do.

Life continued on like that for me, never sure of who I was, and always looking for some kind of stability. I was constantly searching to fill the void that I had inside. Now I had no chance of having a future since I would not be going to college. It really was okay, because I was not even sure of what I'd be going to college to study anyway. I just knew all the other kids I hung out with in high school had college plans, and it seemed that is what their parents wanted for them. They wanted them to go to school and become successful. I, on the other hand, was just lost. I was not sure what was to come next for me. My mother letting my grandpa know that I would not be going anywhere he wanted me to go. She really put her foot down on the matter. He was really hurt by that. She began to act like he was not welcomed to have any input where I was concerned. My dad and her fought about child support for my brother all the time. I think since Mom was not with Dad anymore to help him with his money, he had a harder time keeping track of it. That hurt him, and we lost contact pretty much after that. I was not prepared for anything, and I was now eighteen years old. I remembered at this point starting to hang out with other kids who were not college bound, and even some kids who were a year under me. I began to just want to go out a lot. My mom was not around, and my brother was doing his own thing. Once Mom and Dad divorced, Dad never came around anymore much either.

COULD THIS BE LOVE?

I met Mike when I was eighteen. I was working at a department store, teaching gymnastics, and going to the community college. I met him at a dance club in Collinsville. The girls could be eighteen to get in, but the guys had to be twenty-one. If you were twenty-one, you wore a bracelet that allowed you to drink alcohol. I went with one of my wild friends, wearing next to nothing, and hooked up with Mike. Mike was really the first white guy I actually dated. I had been with white guys sexually on the down low, but not for any kind of real relationship. One week we met, and the next we were sleeping together. Yep, I was falling in love once again. He was from a small town about an hour away, and went to college at a university that was about two hours away. He was much laid back and very sweet. He was all I could think about every day. I could hardly get through the week without seeing him. He would come and visit, and we'd get a motel room and hang out an entire weekend. When it was time for him to go back to school, I found myself spending weekends with him at his college apartment, partying, and having a good time. I would have such a good time with Mike, and then literally get depressed when I had to come back home to the apartment with my mom and brother.

I hated sharing a room with my mother. I found the weekends with Mike stretching out to weeks, and then before I knew it, we were living together. I moved in with him and his two other male roommates. At this point, Mom was not as interested in what I did anymore. She may have felt she did all she could and now the rest of my life was up to me. There definitely was a disconnection now. She worked nights, and she was trying to go back to school to complete her nursing degree. She had put it off so many years to spend her time with us kids. I really felt like moving in with Mike was the next step for my life. I had no real desire to do anything at college. I really was not interested in what my career plans would be. I never even had an idea of what it was I wanted to do when I grew up. I moved in with Mike and was able to get away from my mom. I was able to get a job teaching gymnastics. I was thankful for my background in gymnastics. Mom got me started in acrobats at an early age, then I started gymnastics as I got older. I taught gymnastics when I turned eighteen. I was such an enthusiastic and dedicated worker, but by now my old car was not running the best. Sometimes it would break down, and I would be late for classes. The owner of the gymnastics club helped me by cosigning for me to get a brand new car. I arranged the payments out of my paycheck. This was yet another generous thing someone had done for me. By the time I was driving back and forth to be with Mike, I had a new car. Once I decided to move, I continued to send payments in.

When I moved in with Mike to the small college town, I still did not fit in. The town people who lived in the college town, we called townies. This was in college town, so the townie girls had never encountered anyone like me, black on the outside but white on the inside, so to speak. I was able to make some really close friends, but I had to push past barriers and prove myself, all with no idea of who I was. I taught gymnastics and dance to the little country kids, and they really took a liking to me. It was another story dealing with their parents; some would only see color and none of the talent or ability I had to teach their kids something. I was in an interracial relationship, which had more controversy than ever at that time. Mike was from a small town where being friends with the blacks was okay, but you just did not marry them.

His family did accept me for the most part; after all I did not "act black," right? I was different; I really was like them. I was so good at being whatever people needed me to be.

His mother warmed up to me after some time. His sister and I got along right off the bat. She was sixteen at the time; I was only eighteen when I first met her, and so I could still speak her language. I would ride with her in the car while she had her driver's permit. No one else would ever want to take the time to ride with her, but I always would. She would drive all over town, and we would talk about what was new in her life. She was a very sweet girl, and she liked me just the way I was. She was a cheerleader in the small town, so I would help her with her cheer moves and gymnastics. Mike's brother was always so funny, and we got along great too.

We had our son, Blake, in 1991. When he was born, it seemed all the color walls faded between our families. He was the first grandchild, and that was all that mattered. I was so happy to be a mother. It only seemed right for Mike and I to get married after that, so we did. We got married at the courthouse not long after the birth of our son. We had his brother and a friend of mine from work stand up for us. We spent the weekend at the Holiday Inn for our honeymoon while my mother came and stayed with Blake. My mom always did like Mike, but when she heard we were going to get married, she said to me that she never intended me to marry a white man. Really? That only evoked more confusion. I did find my identity in being a wife and a mother. That void was finally filled with something. My son, Blake, was everything to me. He made me smile every day. He was a good sleeper and an excellent eater. I put my all into being a good mother. It came very natural to me, being a mother. I breastfed my son, and at that time, everyone around me—including my mother—thought that was weird. I had no problem getting up with him for feedings and diaper changes. My sleep cycle changed in order for me to keep up with him. I used to have to always sleep in before I had Blake. I was a person who required large amounts of sleep.

I worked part-time teaching gymnastics and dance, so I was able to spend time with my son. Mike was always very good with money. We lived on a very strict budget, and I was always fine with that. He was very smart about money. I did not feel the need to ever have branded clothing. That was entirely my mother's doing. I was fine with shopping at the thrift store, and mostly I only wore T-shirts and jeans if I was not in workout clothing.

Mike graduated college and eventually we moved back to my hometown. We got an apartment we could actually afford, and life was really good. We were a young couple with our future ahead of us. When it got shaky in my marriage with Mike, we had another child. This child, to my mind, would help reseal the bond and commitment I made to Mike. My daughter, Layla, was born. I remember being so happy to have a little girl to dress up. She was such a great baby with the chubbiest legs you ever saw. Her eyes were somewhat slanted, so strangers would think she was Asian. She had jet-black straight hair. There were times I would panic about how I would be able to raise this child to be a woman without going through all that I had went through.

My grandpa was thrilled to be a great grandpa to the kids. He would come over, bringing the kids gifts, and we would stop by his house every once in a while. He liked Mike and was happy to see I was happy. Layla and Blake are Twenty-three months apart. We now had a boy and a girl. Blake was always with Mike; they were extremely close. Mike would show him how to shoot basketball hoops. Mike loved basketball, and so did his son. Everything evolved around shooting hoops. We had a nerf hoop in every room, and Blake would shoot on demand. Layla loved everything to do with Minnie mouse and stuffed animals. She would line them up and read books to them. Her hair grew to be wavy and long; it was beautiful. Since they were biracial children, they were extremely beautiful and somewhat unique in the area of town where we lived. It was funny because neither one of my kids looked like me, so everyone would always think I was the babysitter or something. It was ironic that I would have biracial children with all the inner turmoil I had with race and who I really was. It was like I could see myself in my children—unique, being both black and white. They were so precious that I could not believe that they came from me. I was so blessed and did not even realize it.

I got word that my grandpa was getting sick. I did not know how to really react to that. I had a hard time with sickness, death and dying over the years. I would sort of shut my eyes to it. Grandpa was now a deacon in the Catholic Church. He had taken all the classes and was really proud. That was the last accomplishment he had made before he became ill. He had Scleroderma and he had been sick off and on for a few years. He was now in the hospital and they had to amputate his leg due to some complications he was having. I went to see him, but I did not stay long. He was in good spirits because he had faith in God, and he knew where his final destination was in the Kingdom of Heaven. I was trying to keep it together. I told him I would be back to see him, and that I would bring the kids. I kissed him on the cheek and left. I will never forget it was Memorial Day and Mike and I had planned to go see him, but for some reason I did not go. He died before I was able to get the kids back to the hospital to see him. I felt crushed but I just shoved those feelings deep down inside me somewhere. I have not really thought about how I felt about his death before writing it at this moment. I had this incredible way of shoving feelings somewhere and just moving on. It was a shrewd way to be but it was how I coped.

Grandpa was the only person on this Earth that showed me real, pure, unconditional love. He showed it to me and to others all around him. Since he was a deacon in the church his funeral was very ceremonial. They had the incense and they wheeled his coffin into the church with all the catholic officials walking beside it in a formal processional fashion. There was a funeral mass service. It was held in St. Peter's church in Kirkwood. This church is gorgeous, very majestic in its architecture and design. This was the perfect place to honor my grandpa. The ceremony had all the prayers and all the formalities the church required. Plenty of the catholic heads of the church were all there. The church was filled with people. Mike was there as my husband comforting me, but I know he could have never imagined the full weight of what I was going through during that time. There was so much I did not share with him surrounding this situation.

Many of the people at the funeral knew exactly who I was, and some did not. I was not mentioned anywhere in the service or listed anywhere on the program. That was very hurtful for me. They had a section of time set aside for people to come up and say a few words. Something tugged at my heart to stand up and take a turn, but I just could not do it. That part made it really sad for me; I just sat there silently and cried. I knew I was his grandchild, and I am sure many there had no doubt since I looked exactly like my father. We had the same nose and the very same smooth mocha brown skin. As I mentioned before, my own father did not even know who I was. It is very ironic; my biological father would hit on me at the wake, showing love to me like I was a piece of meat, and my grandpa only ever showed me the true love of God. There was a war raging for my destiny from the very start, and I never even realized it. My father's sister was there; she was always very pleasant to me. She did acknowledge me. She did not live in the immediate area, so I had not seen her in a very long time. She did not have any kids either, so the family line lives through me and my children.

Something happened to me the day we buried my grandpa. I felt like all hope for me was lost. I longed to be loved like he loved me. I remembered getting a sunflower at Grandpa's gravesite from one of the floral arrangements. It was the one flower that truly reminded me of him. I dried it out and kept it over the years. To this day, sunflowers are my absolute favorite flower. They remind me of how wonderful my Grandpa Jones was not just to me, but to everyone who ever knew him.

Sometime after he died, my grandma contacted me. She wanted to get a paternity test done. It was my guess she needed to settle all her doubts she had over the years. As you can imagine, my mother was highly offended. We found out back then a test like that would cost about five thousand dollars. They would use my hair and something from my grandmother. My father was not a part of any of this. I was ready to go through with it—and then something happened, and we never got the test done. My mother was so disgusted that after all these years, Grandma would try to pull something like this. Mom thought it may have had something to do with my grandpa leaving some money for me or something. Not long after this, Grandma died, so I have no idea what ever happened. I never got anything if he did leave something for me. I do believe that he did leave me something because I was the love of his life, and he was a constant giver. Even though I did not receive any monetary inheritance from him, I know now in writing this story as a believer in Christ I received so much from him when he was alive as a constant light in my life.

Rest in peace, Grandpa Jones. I will see you in a little while, and I will be bringing all your grandkids with me. I will forever love you.

Our little family would always attract attention everywhere we went. Sometimes it was positive attention, and other times negative. My heart was filled with love for my children, yet I was still growing to be very empty and unhappy. I remember my mother telling me that she was shocked at how good of a mother I was.

For some reason, I guess she thought I would not be any good at it. That remark hurt, but I was not surprised by it. I am so amazed at the power of words. The negative things that were told to me over the years just stuck, and I carried them with me.

My mother was very excited to be a grandmother. She took pride in being so young and in good health to be able to do things with her grandkids. She would come and get the kids and take them to church. She did not like the fact that Mike and I did not go to church. I felt as though it was hypocritical for people to go just because it's right to go. The people I knew who went to church acted one way in church, but then were completely something else when church was over. Mike felt the same way, so we never did go. It made my mother happy to take the kids whenever she could, and that was fine with us.

Mike was a good father to our kids, and he was the best husband he could be to me. He had a little bit of insecurity, and he did not always trust me. I found myself having to constantly build him up and also defending myself. Reassuring him that I loved him, and I did not want anyone else. We would argue at times about his putting family first when it came to wanting to party and play golf with his friends. He was a young father and a husband—all of this was an adjustment that came on very fast.

We bought our first house in St. John, and that was exciting for a while. We got a really good deal on a house that had been on the market for over a year. Mike was doing everything to try and make me happy. There was nothing he could do to fix what was broken within me. I was hurting deep down, and nothing could plug the wound in my heart. Every time I thought things would get better, there it was again, that same pang deep down, a longing for something that nothing around me could fill. All I could do is complain about everything that was around me. I was not satisfied with anything. I once again became selfish and started doing more things for me. I went back to school started drifting away from my husband. Since I was now in school around younger kids, I started acting that way to fit in. I was in my mid twenties, but I looked like a teenager, even though I had two kids and a husband at home. My behavior deteriorated from there. It was like I was a childish fool trying to fit in again. When would this cycle end? I had a terrific husband and two fantastic kids, and yet I felt like I needed something else.

I was still teaching gymnastics at this time, and I was also coaching a cheer squad with a really good friend who lived next door to us. He was funny, and we had a blast working together. He really knew cheerleading and gymnastics, so the squad I helped him with was really good. We traveled for different competitions. This, along with school, was pulling me away from my family. During the years I coached gymnastics and cheerleading, Layla and Blake were with me most of the time. The kids I coached on the teams loved my kids. We went as a family down to Florida for a cheer competition, so there were times I could incorporate my family with my career. But before long, I felt like a caged bird. I felt like I had so much potential but no idea what for. The life I had grew stale because of my selfishness, and I needed something else. I eventually asked for a divorce.

The process of divorce was horrible. I remember going to court and seeing Mike there with his mother. I was there with my mother. I felt like a super huge jerk. I had not seen him in months. Was I making a mistake, could I call the whole thing off? By this time, I was already dating and hanging out doing my own thing, and that felt like the right thing. Mike had visibly lost a lot of weight and looked just awful. I was the woman whom he had given everything to, and I just sucked the life out of him and kept on moving. It was like I knew he would be okay, but I needed something to make myself be okay with all of this.

Love is more than just a feeling you lose. It is a choice. I did not know God's love, so I attached my own experiences onto it, which were all wrong. God's love is not selfish, and it endures.

Blake and Layla were ages five and seven. Mike was devastated, and it took him a while before he could even face the kids after we split. He said that if he was not a husband, he could not be a father. In some way, I think he thought he was failing his kids by not being able to make it work with me. None of this was ever his fault. He tried to love a woman who was lost long before he met her. I was a mess going from one thing to the next, with no regard for anyone. Once I made my mind up to leave, that was it. I had no remorse at the time about what I was doing or how my action would affect other people. I only cared about how things affected me. I was extremely selfish. Mike, I am sorry I hurt you. Thank you for loving me and giving me the best of everything you had to offer. I hope you can one day forgive me.

ANOTHER CHANCE AT LOVE?

I went head first right into another relationship, dragging my two kids along. Nothing had changed within me; I was still looking for love, feeling terribly empty, still no idea who I was. Despite all the red flags that were glaringly evident, I just hitched myself to someone else whom I thought I could find my identity in. I had started working out, only to go farther down the road of vanity. I took a lot of pride in the way that I looked, and I loved the attention I would get everywhere I went. I dated a guy who worked at the gym for a little while. He was very much only interested in my body and how I looked. That began to really be the focus of my attention. I would think, *I look good, so I need to find my purpose in that. Maybe I could be a model or even a stripper.* I had no idea who I was or what my talents were. I only knew how to put on a show on stage, all the dance recitals and dance contests I was in over the years groomed me for that, right? I found myself not able to believe the person I was with. He had a very complicated situation with baby mamas, and he even had a baby on the way with another woman when we were dating. It was a web of dysfunction, and eventually, I left the relationship.

I then met Jack. He was tall, in great shape, and very good-looking. I got bold and left my phone number with the girl at the front desk at the gym, and told her to tell him it was mine. I had the habit of being forward with men; I always approached them. I had dated some after the divorce. All were only interested in my body since that was really all I ever had to offer anyone. It took Jack about two weeks, but he finally called me.

I was living in the house that Mike and I had bought, barely able to pay the bills. I had to quit taking classes. I got a job in the collection department at a major department store. I was working full time hours and some evenings. This was a real wake-up call for me. I was now running the household without a man in the house. Mike had gotten an apartment in Edwardsville, so he did not live close by. He would meet me to get the kids every other weekend, and he was paying child support. I was far behind on the house payment and the car payment. All this pressure I had now made me feel like I needed a man to help me. I was feeling like I could not make it on my own; I knew now I had made a big mistake.

The night of our first official date out, Jack and I went to a movie. It was my weekend without the kids. I got a call from Mike during the date I was on with Jack. He was telling me that Layla may have broken her leg and that they were at the hospital. I let Jack know I had to leave. He insisted that he drive me to the hospital since it was in Marion, about forty-five-minute drive. I allowed him to drive me, and once we got there, I insisted he stay in the car. Jack disregarded my wishes—red flag #1; I set a boundary, and he disregarded it. Jack came in with his massive appearance in the crowded small town hospital emergency room. Mike was immediately intimidated. Mike was a very kind and gentle man with a lot of insecurities of his own. I left my relationship with him because I was selfish, and he needed someone who would constantly build his ego. He always accused me of wanting other men in his circle of friends and even his brother at one time. So that, mixed with Jack's massive appearance, was not a good thing. The first word under Mike's breath when he saw me was "bitch." He was hurt that I brought my boyfriend into a family matter. I completely understood that was wrong. Jack heard the comment and immediately chimed in defending me. He started going off on Mike about him calling me a name. There was another red flag: uncontrolled anger. My child needed me, and this was not the time or place for this. I was furious. At this time, I had Lalya in my arms. She was five at the time. She was scared and in pain. I just held her tight and shook my head.

Before long, Mike went to the bathroom and Jack followed him in there. Next thing I heard was a scream from some lady seated near the restrooms. Apparently, something happened in there and somehow a wall got damaged. The police were called. For some reason, Jack was upset, and he thought Mike broke Layla's leg since he smelled beer on Mike's breath. Mike drank beer on occasion, but I knew that had no impact on why our child's leg was hurt. Mike was always good to me and both of our kids, and that never even crossed my mind. The fact that Jack had the audacity to even suggest that made my stomach turn. Jack had way overstepped here, and that was obvious. In fact, what actually happened was Layla was sitting on the floor with a blanket over her legs, and her brother jumped off the couch onto her leg, not knowing where it was under the covers. So here we all were, what in the world was going on?

The police came to the hospital and arrested Jack. Mike did not press charges, but the hospital wanted Jack for destruction of property. Meanwhile, Layla's leg had not been looked at, and there we sat. What a mess. The police told me I would need to bail Jack out that night since it was Friday, or he would be in jail till Monday. I should have let him sit in jail, but no, I called my brother and his wife to come and take Layla to the children's hospital while I worked to get one hundred dollars in cash to the jail somewhere in Illinois to bail that fool out. Not sure why I put that man before my child—worst mistake I ever made at that time, and I continued to make mistake after mistake like that until I found Christ.

Jack, like my mother, was the oldest of nine kids. He took care of his younger brothers and sisters. It was only his mother in the household; no father was ever around much. He often explained to me how awful it was for him. He had story after story about how messed up his childhood was. I would feel so bad to hear the kinds of things he went through. At the same time, it was like he told the stories as if to brag about all he had overcome. But had he really overcome anything? His childhood was a stark contrast to how I was raised with both parents working to give me the best of everything, but not so far off from what my mom's childhood was like. I am sure his mother meant well for her children, but she was the same as all of us were—carrying around past hurts that were never healed. I know that these past hurts were the core to the behavior I experienced being with him in our relationship, and I had those same hurts I was carrying around too. I am a compassionate person, and at the time, I just wanted to hold him and make him forget about his past and look to a brighter future together.

I was working in the collections department for a major department store. We were living in a small three-bedroom slab home. Layla was in a wheelchair. She broke her tibia and needed no surgery, but her entire leg was put in a cast. I took a FMLA leave of absence from work to take care of her. After spending time at home with her and away from that job, I really did not want to return to my job in the collections department. I was calling people trying to collect payment on their charge card. Meanwhile, I was on the other end of the phone with unpaid bills just like them. After the divorce, the house Mike and I purchased underwent foreclosure, and I was having a hard time making ends meet. But there I was once again, being something I was not. I decided not to go back to my job after the leave was over. I was always working out, so I thought I would try to get a job at a gym. I filled out an application at the all-women's fitness club up the street from the house. I was hired and started working in January 1999.

I continued to date Jack and before long, I got pregnant. I remember wanting to have Jack's baby. He did not have any kids, and something made me think that if he had his own, it would soften him around the edges more, so to speak. I was working full time in fitness when I got pregnant with Chloe.

Blake and Layla were growing up so fast. They were doing really well in school, and they had lots of friends. They were never in any trouble. Layla loved to read, so she was always reading out loud to everyone. We'd ride down the road, and she would read every sign she could see. She also was a huge animal lover. She really loved pets. We had a cat when Mike and I were together, and the cat had six baby kittens. Layla took the time to name all of the kittens, and she would care for each of them just like she was their second mama. Blake really liked to skateboard. He was constantly riding outside doing the latest trick he had learned. They were both excited to be big brother and sister soon.

One morning, when I was home from work, I felt a gush down low. I called the doctor, and they wanted me to come in to make sure it was indeed amniotic fluid. I remember paging Jack to let him know, but that day he left his pager at home. I could hear it going off in the house. That just made me furious. He worked construction during the day, so there was really no way to get a hold of him. I went on into the doctor's office. They checked me, and yes, it was amniotic fluid. I was not due until October 13th, and this was only the week before Labor Day!

My doctor told me to go straight to the hospital from his office, so I did. Still no word to Jack about what was happening. I got to the hospital and was admitted right away. I called my mother, and then I was able to call the office at Jack's job to get a hold of him. He got to the hospital not long after that. I was not having any contractions, so that was a good thing. The baby would need to stay in as long as possible since it was too soon for her to be here. I was really scared. My other birth experiences were perfect natural births, and both Blake and Layla took very well to breastfeeding. This whole thing threw me for a loop. That night, my amazing doctor came to check on me. He told me that he wanted to see how long he could keep me from having contractions. I had a bed pad underneath my bottom so the nurses could come in and change the pad every hour. There was a constant flow of fluid coming out. Every time the baby would move, I'd feel a gush. I had an IV with antibiotics to keep me from getting an infection.

The doctor explained that the fluid would constantly replenish itself and not to worry. He told me that I would be confined to the bed and could only get up to use the portable potty that was right next to the bed. I asked how long it would be. He said it could be days or weeks. The longer the better, he said. We need her lungs to be ready. He said he would check the fluid to see how mature her lungs were the next day. Laying there in that bed, I blamed Jack for all of this, for some reason. Of course, he did nothing deliberate, but I felt that because of him, I was here—scared and worried if my baby would make it. I sent him back to the house to get all my stuff. He understood that it was now a waiting game. He planned on staying by my side the entire time. That was huge for him because he never liked missing work.

I was really amazed at how Jack comforted me despite my bad attitude toward him. This was his first baby, and he was really worried about me and the baby. My mom took care of Blake and Layla for us. She came and stayed at our house and made sure they got to school. I was in the hospital for a week. That Labor Day weekend, my doctor was scheduled to go out of town, and I hoped the baby would stay in until he got back. Jack was amazing during this time. Every morning, he would call into work to let his boss know that nothing happened yet, and he would not be in. He was worn out, sleeping in the hospital recliner night after night. Sometimes he would leave to go home and shave and change clothes, but it was not too often. I could see the love in his eyes that he had for me. I could also see the worry and the guilt. He felt like nothing ever went right in his life; it was as if he thought his life was, in some way, cursed.

My doctor made it back the day after Labor Day, and the contractions hit. He checked the fluid, and her lungs were ready. I was in labor for about five hours. It was all natural. God gave me an extremely high tolerance for pain, which really is ironic. Jack was amazing with rubbing my back and keeping me calm and everything. It was awesome to see him in that mode. Three pushes and Chloe was out. She was a preemie, so she had lanugo on her face and body. She was very pale and super tiny. I remember Jack crying when he saw her. He went with her when they took her to get cleaned up. She was brought back to me to nurse. She did not take to my breast at all. Her suck was still premature; I was heartbroken. We tried and tried. She would not even take anything from the bottle either. Jack was devastated. Our daughter would not eat. We were in stress mode again. Jack was thinking about his need to get back to work, as well as being concerned our baby was not eating.

Late that night, the nurse came in and told me Chloe was having some trouble breathing, and they were going to need to watch her closely. Jack had gone home for the night. She brought Chloe in the room in this encapsulated crib. This woman asked if I minded if she prayed for me and my daughter right then and there, and I said, "Please pray." This woman, a stranger on the nursing staff, said the most beautiful prayer over me and my daughter. That night, I cried. Jesus in disguise, I had just experienced the body of Christ reaching out to me. I did not know it then, but there it was. Then it dawned on me—this was the same hospital my grandpa died in years ago. I began to cry. Hours later, they brought Chloe back to me, and she latched on to my breast and was eating with no problem whatsoever. That was the power of prayer in action. That woman was a believer, and God interceded on her behalf because *he* had a calling on my life that I was completely unaware of. She acted out on her faith and was being obedient to Christ, thus planting a mustard seed of faith in my heart. Prayer is powerful; I did not know anything about that then, even though I saw it in action. I was still very blinded by darkness.

Jack was so excited to see our girl eating when he came back early that morning. He kissed me on the head and went off to work. Chloe was going to be just fine. She had lost some weight since birth because she had not eaten much. She was weighing four pounds, eight ounces. They needed her to weight five pounds before we could take her home. She was able to gain the weight, and we were able to go home within a few days.

It felt good to be home after such a long time in the hospital. I really missed Blake and Layla. Getting back home to them was all I wanted to do. I was excited to be a mother to three children. Chloe was jaundiced, so I had to make sure she got adequate sunlight during the day. Blake and Layla were so helpful and excited to have a baby sister. My mom came over with her husband, Fred, to visit and to see Chloe. Jack was very adamant that Blake and Layla did not touch the baby, or even get too close to her since she was a preemie. And after all the stress we went through to get her here, he was overly concerned they would hurt her.

My mom was holding Chloe at the time, and the kids were much too close to her than Jack would allow, so he cautioned them to get back. It was obvious they were only trying to bond with their sister. When Jack was gone at work during the day, I allowed the kids to hold the baby and help me with her, so I knew they were fine with her. My mom said, "Jack, its okay. They are not going to hurt her. That is just silly what they say in the hospital. It is good for babies to bond with their families. I am a nurse, so I know these things. The kids' hands are clean, so stop worrying." Jack verbally exploded on my mother, yelling at her and telling her to get out of our house, and that what he has to say about his baby is what matters. He used expletives and slammed the door when she left. Before Mom got to the door, she looked at me and said, "See what you've gotten yourself into?" This was the same behavior that he displayed at the hospital when Layla's leg was broken. I cried for hours after this, probably because I was a homornal mess since I had just given birth. I was in an awful, awful situation being with this man; I could feel it in the pit of my stomach. Reflecting back on this now—and it is a very weird thing—no one had ever stood up to my mother like that before, and for some reason, after the dust settled from that incident, she sort of had a newfound respect for Jack.

Months after Chloe was born, Jack and I got married. We flew to Las Vegas for the weekend and had a small ceremony with just the two of us. I wore a wedding dress, and he had a tuxedo. We had a limo and a cake and flowers and a photographer. The only thing missing was friends and family members. We did not want any input from anyone from either side of our families. Mom came and stayed with the kids for the weekend. She was always there to help me when I needed her for the kids. I was happy for the most part. Jack was an excellent provider, and he would do anything for his family, which was obvious. I felt safe with him, like nothing could ever hurt me. It was like he set those boundaries I needed in my life at that time. He kept me tethered. My family was complete.

Chloe began to look more and more like me as she grew. She now had a cocoa completion like mine, and she had her father's chin and jawline. She would grow to be a very sickly baby. She would have trouble breathing more and more as she grew. She was first hospitalized at six months old. She had bad asthma, but she was so young they never would diagnose her as such. She was on lung steroids and also used a bronchial nebulizer at this young age. She would have problems at least once every couple of months. She was still a very good baby even with all her medical issues. She was always a good sleeper and a good eater. She would rarely fuss when it came time to take her medications.

IS THIS WHO I AM?

At the same time I was doing it all—wife, mother, full-time job—I had found a love in the career of fitness. I was good at sales because I could get along with anyone. Whether it was a younger white girl, or a middle-aged black or white woman, I knew how to be what they needed me to be, so, needless to say, I could sell fitness memberships. Fitness management is a sales management position. My numbers in sales are what got me into management. I was beautiful and in great shape for having three kids, so the women really liked me. I was an assistant manager at a women's health club, and I was trying to be mom to three kids. I finally found myself in a career I was good at. I do credit that to Jack, since he was the one who told me I would be good at it. I see it as such a strong parallel now. I was good at it because he told me I'd be good at it.

Words play such a huge part in our development. It really matters to us what people whom we care for say about us. It develops our belief systems about ourselves, be they good or bad.

The problem now was that I was barely there for my kids since I worked three nights a week until 9 p.m. This meant Jack would have to take care of the kids on the evenings I would be gone. This also meant the kids did not have any regular extracurricular activities—so different from how I was raised. Layla and Blake were intimidated by Jake. He was a large and intense man. Jack would comment that I treated my kids like privileged kids, and they never would learn to do anything on their own since I'd do most things for them. They would stay in their room until I got home and put them to bed. Blake would tell me that he was scared to ask Jack for dessert, and he and his sister would fight over who would ask him. They were really good kids; I was really blessed. I would continually defend his behavior to my kids, even when I knew deep down that his approach to discipline was often just wrong. After all, he was just doing what he knew to do. He did not have a loving father around, so how could he be one? Baby Chloe was left in her swing or her activity seat the entire time I was gone.

Jack was a computer gamer. It was awful the amount of hours he would spend playing an online fantasy game of some sort. I believe this was his way of dealing with a hurtful childhood and escaping the current stresses of life. He did not drink or smoke, but he did have addictive behavior when it came to computer gaming. He always looked down on others who had chemical additions, but he did not realize his own addiction.

Many of us have addictions to things we may think are insignificant if they are not as obvious as drug or alcohol usage. Too much of anything in order to mask pain or fill a void is just as harmful.

I was burning the candle at both ends, and for a while, that kept me oblivious to the pain I was going through. I put everything into the clients I was working with. I have always had an immense compassion for others more so than those related to me. I took interest in wanting to do more than just sell memberships. I wanted to be more involved in the service part of fitness. I wanted to be a personal trainer, and teach the fitness classes and not just get women excited, signed up, and then send them on their way. I felt like they were buying me. It was because of how I made them feel that prompted them to join the fitness club; so I wanted to be a part of their success.

Being a manager at the gym I worked for, you either did sales management or service, and not both. There were only a couple people in the entire corporation that did both. My boss was one of those people. Angel did it all. She was the manager, and I was her assistant. She taught classes, sold memberships, and she was a personal trainer. She had been in the fitness business since she was a very young adult. She was a mentor to me, and I wanted to follow her lead. I went to her and told her what I wanted to do. She saw potential in me but warned me about possible burn out and reminded me that I did have three kids at home to consider. She especially worried for Chloe, who was still so sickly. She would still need forty hours in sales from me, and the classes and training sessions would be extra. She arranged for the company to pay for my personal training certification and my group fitness certification also. I had arrived; I was now really doing it all!

During the time I worked at the womens fitness club, God surrounded me with all kinds of wonderful women whom I have remained friends with over the years. It was a time in my life were I saw hope in the power of being a woman. I talked boldly about sex; I developed a crass sense of humor. I was even more prideful about having a great body after having three natural childbirths. So wrapped in pride, I got a breast augmentation, since the three kids left a lasting impression on my breasts. Jake was shocked I saved the money, scheduled the surgery, and had it done. It was a time in my life I learned to set goals and reach them, and felt empowered doing so. I would be the one to always say what others were thinking but would never say for themselves. I would work with clients who wanted to join the gym but would need approval from their husbands, or they were doing it to gain approval from their husbands. I would always think to myself and express to other coworkers that will never be me. I will never let a man control me like that. There were older women I worked with and younger girls as well. We all grew so close over the years we formed a sisterhood like no other. These women helped me to laugh and grow to learn many different things about myself.

I also encountered the body of Christ reaching out to me in the form of a client I had named Francine. She was an older Christian woman whom I took an interest in right away. She was always so positive and very easy to talk to. She was very conscious about her health since she was older. She did not look as old as she said she was. We became very close. She was very active in her church, and she loved to save money. She would bring me coupons for diapers and baby things I would need for Chloe. She had invited Layla and I to her church for a mother-daughter tea and spring fashion show they had once. She had also invited us to her house on many occasions. She loved the Lord, and so did her husband, Philip. There it was again—God's love being shown to me through this woman and her husband, and yet I kept on doing things my way, never even realizing that the love they knew was for me to know also.

It immerged that Chloe would have a learning disability at age three, and that caused more stress on the marriage. Was it all the medications she had been taking at such an early age? That question was always at the back of my mind. Chloe could understand what was being said to her, but she could not express herself with words. She would get so angry she would throw herself down and start banging her head on the ground. She was initially diagnosed with language impairment, as well as behavioral disorders labeled as ADHD. I was made to think that she did not have a disability, that is was the way I was raising her. I think Jack was in denial, and I was made to feel guilty for focusing so much on my career. I carried tremendous guilt because of my work schedule and the fact that she was in daycare full-time. At this point, I could not just quit; we needed the money I was bringing in. I was able to stay home with Layla and Blake during their preschool years, so I felt guilty I could not do the same for Chloe.

I had earned all kinds of awards and trips in fitness. Angel had it arranged that I would be the trainer to the St. Louis Ram's cheerleaders, the year after they won the super bowl. I would work with some of the girls one-on-one in the gym, and then as a group at the practice stadium in Earth City once a week. It was an awesome privilege to do that. I also had the honor of working with a couple of female radio hosts. The gym I worked for was named their official sponsor for the cheerleaders, and they had air time purchased on several radio stations. Angel even nominated me as one of the area's fittest moms to be featured in a local magazine. She believed in me, and I felt like I found myself with new my career, but I could not find balance between my job and my home life. I was withdrawing more and more from my family life. I wanted to party and hang out with the girls I worked with. I was able to do that quite a bit. Jack did not mind, since he would rather be on the computer, and he did not drink alcohol anyway; he also knew all the girls I worked with, and that kept him at ease. I was looking for an escape from the responsibility I had at home to my kids and to my husband. The time I was spending away from home and working so much was of course putting a strain on our marriage. I was feeding a party lifestyle and starving my home life. It seemed the tethering I so desired in the beginning of the relationship was beginning to feel like a noose. The protective husband thing I felt comfort in before began to suffocate me. These things pushed me away.

It was a natural law at work- feed what you want to grow, starve what you want to die.

Within a year of Chloe's diagnosis, I asked for a divorce. We had been married almost four years, and I felt like our marriage was beyond repair and I had other interests—none of which were about trying to make it work. Jack was begging me to stay with him, and promised that things could get better, but I felt like I was married to an alien. We could not communicate effectively, so everything he would say to me made me mad. He was so irritating to me; I just wanted out of the marriage. I found out I was pregnant right after I had decided I wanted out of the marriage. I knew that I could not raise another child with a person like Jack—plus, I was already too busy for the children I had. I already had it in my mind set to divorce Jack. Since it was all about me, I saw no other option than to terminate the pregnancy. Jack begged me not to; he said that things could be different between us. He asked me, "Am I really all that bad?" I had my mind made up, and I had interest already in someone else. I was not about making things work; I was all about running on to the next thing to make things better. I was all about blaming someone else, and then moving on to someone else to fill the gap. How long would I continue this cycle? How many times would I circle this same mountain?

God was showing me to look *up* to *him*, but I kept doing my life in my will, creating one disaster after another. A wayward child getting more and more filthy in the mud while my Father waited for me, never growing weary with his arms wide open for me to return.

My mother took me to get an abortion. I do not remember her trying to talk me out of it. She knew I was adamant about my decision. She clearly did not understand God's word about sanctity of life. I do remember that was definitely a time she was there to support me no matter what. Before the procedure, they did an ultrasound and told me I was six weeks along. I asked to see the ultrasound since I had seen many before. This would after all be the fourth time I was pregnant. What I saw at that time looked like a kidney bean, and somehow that put me at ease with my decision. I was so blinded by darkness and the ways of the world.

Looking back now, I can now see how I affected what God ordained with my selfish act. Every child who is conceived has a purpose. What was the purpose of the child I was *carrying?* What was the purpose of the descendants of that child? How would that child affect others in my family—or the world even? What if my mother would have aborted me and cut off the chance for me to have wonderful children who will do great things? I would have never been here fulfilling my purpose, being used as a vessel to tell my story to reach a hurting world. I mourn the loss of what could have been. I also rejoice in the fact that the God I serve can take such a mess and turn it into a message for someone who needs to hear it.

I am so sorry that I was so selfish, foolish, blind, and ignorant to what God's Word says about the sanctity of life. I am here to tell this story because I am forgiven, and I have received his righteousness as a gift; therefore, *his* precious blood redeems me.

I had the abortion on Friday, and then I was in the divorce lawyer's office on Monday, filing for yet another divorce. Who does that? What was wrong with me? Why was I so selfish? I was in complete darkness and just did not care. I was going to fix things my way and keep moving. After all, I had found power in being a woman.

WILL THIS CYCLE EVER END?

I was with someone else with all my baggage, waiting for my divorce from Jack to be final. It was so easy for me to just go on to the next thing without look back or even taking time to figure out what went wrong. I was not sure what I was running from, but I had to keep moving to keep the façade that everything was okay. I was cracked, broken, and a wreck on the inside; but I looked good, and I could speak well, and that is all that mattered, as long as I did not speak too much about my past. I got engaged to the guy I was dating and thought I wanted to get married, but something had changed in me briefly, and I realized that I was not ready to get married.

I realized this time that I was running from one set of problems right into another. During this time, I felt like I wanted more for my life. I felt like I was special, and I could be successful. I had started going with my brother to different multi-level marketing meetings. I was getting really motivated learning about residual income, working my own hours, and having my own business. I met quite a few successful people and went to various success seminars. I could see a financially fit future for myself. My brother and I were different and very special. We could do public speaking and motivate others around us. We were running meetings and talking to different business leaders in the area; it was another time of growth for my self-esteem in my life. Somewhere I got off-track with the business, and I started to feel the void again, longing to have someone to love me. I was seeing more of the seeds of success planted inside me at this time, but I still did not know God's love for me, so it was cut off while I tried to fill the void where God goes with another person.

God created us for himself. We all have a universal longing inside us that only *he* can fill. We will never have a full and abundant life until we recognize that and invite him in to help us. Without him, we can do nothing.

I was now in another relationship with a man much older than I was. He was a millionaire, and I was definitely attracted to his success. It also seemed he understood what it took to become successful. He understood working hard to pursue a dream and seeing the hard work pay off. He was married but separated, pursuing a divorce. He had many cars, houses, a boat, and a multi-million-dollar home. All he needed was the perfect trophy girlfriend, which was where I fit in. By this point in time, I was labeled the hot black chick with a nice rack. That was disgustingly degrading—didn't anyone see anything more to me than that? I did not mind it at the time. I was so full of pride, but I had no clue who I was.

Things were great at first—I did not have to work, but eventually he had me running his business somewhat. I had no interest in his business, but I was good with talking to people, and I was a pretty face. He would bring me along to help him close different business deals. I gave up personal training because that was not something he really approved of; giving my attention to others was not part of his plan. Why would I give up something God clearly gifted me to do just because a man did not approve? I was blind and could not see.

This relationship is a very painful one to write about because I completely was going against everything that I was to be something completely different for someone else. I was basically molded little by little into what this person wanted me to be, very similar to how I felt in my childhood. I let this happen to myself. I think I was trying to reinvent myself, which is almost impossible when I had no idea who I was in the first place. It was like I was stripped of all the accomplishments I had achieved doing what I loved in fitness. All while being enticed with trips and things. He bought the clothes he wanted me to wear, all very tastefully revealing. Remember, I never was one much for name branded things. My wardrobe has always been simple. Here I was being dressed up again. I had a great body, and that was all it was about. It was like I was just another one of the many shiny things he had. Something others would envy—the hot black chick on this older white man's arm. I knew everywhere we went together, people had to think I was either a hooker or a gold digger or both. Was I these things?

Perception would be their reality. I forced myself to love him—all the while I was losing myself more and more every day. I got this person's name tattooed on my body to try to make myself commit to him mentally on some perverted level. Literally in doing that, I was just branding myself as his and not my own. I tried to make myself see that this was as good as it would get for me.

The kids loved staying in the big house and all; he was never stingy with his money, and he was always good to them. Deep down, I just knew it was all wrong. We were almost engaged, but after a real wake-up call in a near psychotic break for me, our relationship ended, and I moved out. In all of this, his sister, whom I was really close to, gave me a woman's daily Bible and a gospel CD of The Brooklyn Tabernacle Choir. There was the body of Christ reaching out to me once again. But where was my family when I needed them? Did they think I was doing well because I lived in a big house? Could they not see that I was making the same mistakes over and over again? Could they not see I was so lost and hurting with no idea who I was? What was unconditional love? I can remember we had a little dog that we all loved. The dog would always follow me around. I was the one who took care of the dog, made sure she ate and would take her for walks and rides in the car. One morning, it was cold, and I got up to let the dog out. I remembered just wanting a cigarette so bad. I just got up half-dressed and went out. I did not take the time to put the dog on a leash when I let her out with me. I remember it was so cold outside. The dog ran off and so I went back in the house to put some clothes on so I could go run after the dog. My boyfriend got up and asked me what was going on. I told him the dog ran off. He jumped up and went out to get the dog. I remember he came back carrying a lifeless dog in his arms saying she got hit by a car, and he threw the dog on the floor, and I fell to my knees and just held the dead dog. I did not cry, I could not breathe—I am not sure what I felt. I remember my boyfriend at the time saying, "What is wrong with you? The dog is dead, and you are not even crying, it's like you don't even care." I was frozen and in a fog. It was like at that moment, I realized that this was my life, and I need to wake up and make changes. It was as if the dead dog symbolized who I was and where I was headed. Yet I could not really mourn; it was like I was just stuck in a time warp of some sort.

I went to see my regular counselor, and I remember her telling me that she was seeing emerging behavior that she could not help me with. She thought I seemed manic. I was really excited about the holidays and seeing my family, and when I got to her office, I was talking at a super-fast rate, and my thoughts were racing. She said she thought I needed medication, and I needed to see a psychiatrist. This was the first time I did feel like I really wanted to die. I was supposed to see my mom's family that night for a Christmas celebration at Chili's after my appointment. I went straight home and got in the bed and stayed there. Depression hit me hard. Did my family not notice I did not show up for the party? Were they worried about me? Could they have called to see if I was all right? Did they care about me? Have I disgraced them so that all they could do is talk about my failures and not reach out to help me up? Here I was quickly approaching thirty-five, and I kept repeating the same mistakes, and I still had no idea who I was, and no clue as to what love was, and now I *was* crazy.

Before this, I was living with my three kids in my brother's basement. My brother had his girlfriend move in with her three kids. My brother had two kids of his own also. So there were three adults and eight kids in one house. Mike had bought a house in a nearby state, so he now had room for Layla and Blake to have their own rooms. I agreed to change the visitation to where Blake and Layla would spend the school year with their dad, and see me every other weekend and then stay with me during the summer. That was another big mistake I made. The kids developed their roots and friends at their dad's; they had summer activities they did not want to leave, so it was very hard to develop a consistent visitation schedule. Mike was able to get them involved in sports and activities. He was very involved with the kids and sports; he would help out with coaching, and he would be at every game. I commend him for picking up the ball where I had completely dropped it. I was never able to do that for the kids. They enjoyed playing sports, and they were good at them. Since their games and activities would mostly be on the weekends, that would make the visitation schedule hard to adhere to, plus I was always in one relationship or another, circling yet another mountain, filling a void inside me, and not paying attention to what was important.

I would come out and see the kids do their activities. Layla was on the speech team now, so I would come out and listen to her give her speeches. It was awesome to see her speak in front of large crowds. Her father had a real fear of public speaking, so he was especially amazed. Whenever I would come to one of their events at school, their schoolmates would be shocked that their mother was black. Layla and Blake are light, completed with just a hint of bronze coloring, so most kids thought they were white. I remember going to the junior high school one day and dropping in to see Blake. He was with a huge group of his friends, and he literally ran over to me and gave me a huge hug and kiss in front of his friends. I was lucky my kids still loved me very much. There was no resentment toward me for all my foolish behavior. They were also adjusted very well to all the change around them. That was yet another blessing from God.

Meanwhile, Jack had remarried. I had suggested after the divorce that he hire help with Chloe. He did not fully understand her diagnosis, so I wanted to make sure he had someone to be with her during his visitation times. Jack ended up marrying the girl who was helping him with Chloe.

It seemed to me that Jack's new wife was working hard at trying to take my place as Chloe's mother. I am sure he had told her about what a horrible mother I had been and all about my party lifestyle and on and on. All these things were true, so of course, she would feel she would have the upper hand in raising my child, even if I was fifteen years her senior. I was an aloof parent. She would show up at the school IEP meetings for Chloe in place of Jack. I would have to schedule visitation pickups and drop-offs through this woman. She had Chloe in dance class and never told me when the recitals were. She had Chloe's ears pierced without telling me. It was a horrible time for me. Chloe was acting out at school, hitting the principal and spitting on teachers. It was as though Jack replaced me as a mother and a wife. After all, I aborted his child and let my other two kids go live with their father—so why would I want to be a parent to Chloe? Was he right? Is this what I've become, a selfish person with no disregard for anyone but myself? *Yes!* He wanted his new wife to be her mother and for me to sign papers to only see Chloe every other weekend. What in the world was this? I hurt him by leaving, so he was going to punish me? God has the final say in all things.

God stepped in and saved me from myself. I got a call from Jack. He was sobbing, and I could hardly understand him. He told me his wife had died. She overdosed on some pills and died that night at the hospital. He called it an accidental suicide. This should have been yet another red flag, but I blew right past it to rally by Jack's side to comfort him. I felt really sorry for him, like in some way it was my fault. I never stopped to think that *maybe* the poor girl ended her life because of the relationship she was in, which appeared so perfect to me. Jack did have her doing everything he needed her to do, include aiding in trying to take away my child and destroy my life. This is my perception, so it is my reality.

Here I was, back to his side to comfort him. I was doing fine for a short stint, just before this happened. I had not been dating anyone for about a month—that was a long time for me. I did see the psychiatrist, and I was diagnosed with bipolar disorder and depression. The psychiatrist told me not to get into any type of relationship, especially not a physical one. I was taking medication and was feeling better. I was doing really well; I had my own apartment and a job in the fitness industry. I was even doing television on a local public access channel, which my aunt Clara-who always believed in my talents- recommended me for an interview to do a fitness spot. I got the job and was paid to do ten ninety-second fitness inserts on a show that featured a doctor. It was great. I was doing what I loved and trying new things, getting out of my comfort zone—then, I slipped right back into what was comfortable, dysfunctional. That seemed comfortable to me since that was all I knew. We rekindled a courtship a very short time after Jack buried his wife. It was all completely a physical relationship. This was another red flag. That is not enough time for anyone to grieve properly, which means he probably shoved more feelings down deep somewhere within him that only would come back up in some sort of sideways behavior. Hurt people will hurt other people.

The rekindled courtship between Jack and I resulted in the pregnancy of my fifth child, Olivia. I could not believe I was pregnant…*again*! I finished the last couple of fitness shoots for the television station. I remember ignoring phone calls from the producer of the show. I missed a cast party and the chance to meet everyone involved with making the show, including the doctor who was featured on the show. I was falling fast into depression and defeat.

I did not want to be pregnant, but there was no way I was going to take another life into my own hands. I knew I could never carry any more guilt than I already had. So here I was, thirty-seven-years old, pregnant again, with a stunted career path, and in a questionable relationship. I had stopped taking depression medication since I was pregnant. At that time before I got pregnant, I was still a closet smoker. I completely quit that cold turkey when I read positive on the pregnancy test. I worked for a while; I had a few clients. I was pregnant and all I cared about was eating and sleeping.

During this time, my relationship with Chloe grew. She was seeing a counselor regularly and doing play therapy. She was doing much better in school. She went through so much with the divorce of her mom and dad, and then the remarriage of her father and twice engaged mother. On top of not fully understanding why her new stepmom would not be coming back, and now her mom is back with her dad. This child was so resilient in all of this; it was truly amazing to me. She was so positive and happy all the time, despite the confusion. She and I would go out to eat together and watch movies. She had her mommy back, and that was just what she needed. During that time, she was what really kept me going—her positive attitude and her infectious smile. She really loved me despite all my flaws and mistakes. She knew that I was going to have a baby, but I am not sure she really understood what that would really be like. She was seven years old with mental developmental delays. She was just thrilled to have me all to herself.

I lived on my own for as long as I could. Jack had bought a rental house, so I was living there and paying him rent. I moved back into the other house with Jack when I was about seven months pregnant. I was now living with him in the house that he and his wife before me just bought not even a year before. I was the one to clean out all of her belongings after her death. That was just so weird. He did not want to see any of her stuff or even talk about it. There were pictures of the two of them all over the house. It was very painful for me, but I was able to do it. I slept in the same bed they had shared as man and wife in that house. What was I doing?

I did not have any friends, and I was closed off for the most part from my family. I missed Layla and Blake. They would invite me to different things at their school, and I was very hit-and-miss with attendance. Layla had started her period, and I was not around for that. It was a blessing that Layla had her grandma and her aunt around to help nurture her needs as a woman. By now, she was also a daddy's girl and was able to get anything she wanted from him. Mike did not remarry or really have a serious relationship after we divorced. He was really focused on the needs of the kids. I regretted not being there for them. I did not complete the parenting of my older kids, and now I have a seven-year-old with a disability, and I was pregnant with yet another child. I still had no idea who I was. All these things were swirling in my mind. There were many times I wanted my older kids to move back with me. I knew deep down that would not be fair to them. I was in bad shape and so empty with barely anything to give.

I was not physically active anymore, so I found myself on the computer more often. I joined *CaféMom*, an online community for moms. I met quite a few online friends through that site. I joined a group of women who were all due to have baby girls in the month I was due. These women were such a great support to me. I would stay on the computer for hours reading posts of what was going on in everyone's pregnancies. The time came for me to have Olivia. She was born without complication. She looked very much like her father. Jack was there and very supportive, like he was eight years prior when Chloe was born. The labor was not long, and she emerged with about five pushes. Olivia came into this world quietly. She was asleep when she was born. She simply opened her eyes and looked at everyone and took her time before she actually cried. My mother was there in the room with us this time. My doctor said to me, "You're body was made to have babies." Yeah, if he only knew. What I worried about most during my pregnancy was nursing Olivia. How could I do so with breast implants? At the time I had gotten them, I just knew I was done having children. It turns out I was able to nurse Olivia with no problem. *God's grace.* My new hope was to just make everything right. I wanted the girls to have both parents together under the same roof. I just wanted normalcy, but most of all, I wanted peace.

HOW CAN I FIND PEACE?

I pressured Jack into getting married again. At the time, we were getting along about the same as before—we just now had a new baby to focus on. I assured him we could make it. He seemed very distant and was obviously still hurting from the passing of his wife. After being in the previous relationship where I had lost myself completely, being with Jack felt like a much better place to be. It was the better choice of two bad choices. I felt like it was what needed to happen to make things right. I was going to fix yet another mess. I found a marriage officiator online, called, and set a date; and we got married in this woman's apartment for eighty dollars. All the kids were there for the ceremony. I remember Blake and Jack laughing, saying that we just got married by the woman who looked like the oracle from the movie *The Matrix*. That was about the size of it. I was now remarried to the man I had just divorced years prior. Everything was now going to be fine, it just had to be, right? I was wrong!

I wallowed in great depression after the birth of Olivia. I was thirty-eight-years-old, and I did not know who I was. I was extremely overweight and in darkness and pain. I tried to focus everything on my kids. I wanted to redeem myself as a parent.

By this time, Blake and Layla were teenagers doing their own thing and rarely had time to spend with me. I had missed their proms that past year; I was not there for them at all. They never did complain or ever make me feel bad. They knew what kind of stress I was under. It was like they worried for me. They wanted me to always know that they were fine, and that I needed to focus on making things fine for myself. My teenage kids had it all right. They grasped more about life than I ever did at their age. That was a huge blessing.

I remember when they came to visit right after Baby Olivia was born. They drove down and stayed over a night. When time came for them to leave, I cried and cried and cried. It really hurt me deep down that they were leaving me. I was very hormonal since I just had the baby, so that, on top of the fact that I was really hurting, was the reason why I could not stop crying. I wanted all of my babies with me. I wanted to change the past and just start new. I told them I was so sorry over and over. I know they could see my pain; they assured me that they would be back to see me again soon, and to calm down and not worry about them. They told me they loved me, and they wrapped their arms around me to give me that assurance. I did feel better.

Jack would try to put me at ease by telling me I need not worry about them because I now had two girls in the house who desperately needed me. Why I continued to listen to any advice this man had for my life was beyond me.

One day, my mother came over to see baby Olivia. It was obvious I had gained weight, was out of shape, and depressed. I remember sitting by her on the couch, and she said to me, "Well, I guess you are going to be fat like the rest of us now," and she patted me on my leg. She was referring to her and all of her sisters who have struggled with their weight for years. I never had a weight problem, so I took that comment pretty hard. The power of words once again. It lit a fire under my butt to do something to get the weight off. I turned to my online friends on *CaféMom* and found a weight loss group. I connected with many women, but there were three there who really positively impacted me every day I logged on. Beth, Jamie, and Stephanie were blessings that God sent to me through the Internet. We were all struggling to lose weight, and we worked together to help encourage others to lose weight and stay positive along the way. These women were the only real friends I had at the time. They only knew of me what I had shared; they did not judge me in any way. I grew to love these women, and to this day, even though I am still in contact with them, I have never met them face to face.

I went up to the center that was close to the house. I met a very nice young girl there. I got signed up for some workout classes. I started going, and to my surprise, the class size was very scant. It was a nice facility, and the price for classes was very reasonable, but there were less than five participants in the class. I kept coming to class, and I began to eat right, and in six months, I lost sixty pounds. The young girl I met there suggested that I find out about getting a job at the center. She knew that I used to be a personal trainer and a fitness instructor (I often found my identity in being a trainer and instructor). I was starting to feel that role again since I had lost my weight. I filled out an application, and I got an interview.

There, God placed another blessing in my life. Ellen was in charge of the fitness program. She explained that the program was given to her, and she was doing all she could to get it going. She had problems with instructors not showing up for classes, and she needed some fresh class ideas. I was all over that. I knew how to breathe fresh life into the program. I was excited at the opportunity. She hired me right on the spot. I told Jack I had a job. He was not that thrilled about it. I explained that I would work when he could be at home with the kids. At this time, he was laid off and working for a temp service, so he did not have a consistent work schedule. He would spend all his time on the computer, at least fourteen hours a day.

The counselor I had been seeing had told me that she thought that Jack may have some specific behaviors that could be related to a certain personality type. I would often explain situations involving him. She had been my counselor since before we divorced. She had worked with Chloe for some time as well. She told me there was a personality test that he could take online that was very in-depth, and it may help me get more insight on how to communicate better with him, to help us out in our marriage. That was going to be her focus—to help me to be a better wife by understanding the way he thinks. I really thought that could help me, but I was not sure I would ever be able to get him to take the test. Jack and I knew that we both had very strong personalities. He always explained himself as the tether, the immoveable object who was always trying to bring me back to the center. He was right about that—I was all over the place with no anchor in anything but myself. That was a faulty place to have an anchor because I was only a human with countless flaws, and I did not even know who I was!

I did get him to take the online test. He answered over a hundred questions. The testing showed it was very likely he had specific behavioral tendencies. That was not an actual diagnosis, but it gave us something to work within our relationship. It helped things make better sense to him and to me about how he processed information. Jack was a highly intelligent person but had some real quirks about him. This information gave me a better understanding of what I was dealing with. Looking back at past behavior, it explained a lot of things to me. The main things that stuck out were emotional detachment, the lack of being able to be empathetic to the needs of others, using very direct language without use of tact, induced stress level in a change of routine, being obsessed with information, things either being black or white and never gray. I was starting to understand him somewhat. As time went on, it became more like a crutch for him, and he would sometimes use his thinking as an excuse.

I felt better physically, I lost another twenty pounds making my weight loss total eighty pounds lost in eight months. I looked great, but my heart was heavy. I worked with Ellen with the kind of classes I could teach and with the schedule I had. She understood that my husband's schedule would hinder my schedule since we only had one car and that he did not approve of the baby being watched by anyone else. I presented a couple of ideas to her. One idea was a mom and tot stroller class we could offer in the park near my house. That way, I would walk there, and Olivia could come with me. That went over great. I taught that class and then introduced an early morning boot camp that we would try. That went over great also. I worked with a few employees from the center as well. I loved what I was doing. Jack could tell I was gaining my confidence back, which only escalated what seemed like hatred toward me. About this time, he did get a full-time job. It was going to be good money, but the hours would be very awkward for the start.

We argued about Olivia going to the program they offered at the center from 9 a.m. to 12. She was two and now old enough to go. The price was reasonable, and I was not sure why he did not want me to have a break from her. As a baby, Olivia was super clingy and always wanted to be held. I breastfed her, and she slept with me since Jack mostly worked nights. I needed a break! The time I did have away from home was spent nurturing other people to reach their fitness goals. I finally just signed her up and suffered the wrath of him being mad at me and being told that I would leave my child with anyone. Did he not realize that I knew everyone who worked up at the center? I had trained many of them, or they knew me from trying a class I taught. I knew she would be in good hands.

I did not see my family. My brother, mother, and dad did not like Jack, which further enabled him to keep me in a controlled environment. Jack had nothing good to say about anyone in my family and felt I was better off without them around me. He had to have control of his environment at a very early age, so that was all he knew. He had to be the man of the house and protect his younger brothers and sisters, and be mentally available for his mother who was very unstable. When you do not take the time to deal with past hurts, you *will* hurt other people. I was one of those people who was hurt, and I also hurt other people. I knew that the way I was living was not right. Just when things seemed to get better, they would drastically turn for the worst.

Layla and Blake would visit every now and then. They loved seeing their little sisters. It was nice when all the kids would be together. Layla was playing with Olivia and making her laugh when she noticed some small dark wholes in her teeth. She asked me what they were. I had not even noticed them before. It was Easter, so I thought maybe it was some chocolate candy she had in her mouth. I did not think anything more of it. Jack had just started his new job, and we did not have dental coverage yet. So when the coverage did kick in in July, I got Olivia to the dentist. She was about twenty-nine months old. She was a night nurser. She would co-sleep with me since Jack worked nights. She would then nurse off and on throughout the night. I did not realize that would be damaging to her teeth. I really thought breast milk would not cause damage that only baby formula at night would do that.

The dentist explained to Jack and I that her teeth were rotted and would need to be extracted. The tiny pinhole cavities could not be repaired on the baby teeth, and the danger was that this would impact her permanent teeth underneath. This would be done in surgery, and she would be put to sleep in order for it to be done. Jack was really upset, and I know deep down he blamed me. I blamed me that was easy to do. I was crushed as I listened to the doctor. She urged me to stop the night breastfeeding. I assured her that had already stopped for months at that time. All the things in my life that went wrong were my fault, so tacking this on was no problem. We talked about how we were going to pay for the surgery since it was going to be costly but very necessary. Our option was to do a health care card through Jack's work. Once that was set up, we got the surgery scheduled.

We took Olivia in, and she had the surgery in the dental office. The anesthesia team was there to do everything so she would not be in any pain. She was so brave but so small. She had nine teeth extracted. This included four right across the front. Jack and I waited in the waiting room. Once she was in recovery, we got to see her. Her mouth was swollen and red. We got the aftercare instructions and took her home. Her recovery was miraculous; she did so good I was amazed. She had to have liquids, and then we worked up to solids. She was on an antibiotic and had motrin for pain relief. About a month after her surgery, she had a mold made of her mouth, so she was able to get an appliance put in to serve as her front teeth. The appliance was great! She had a beautiful smile once again.

Jack would always hold things I did in my past and present up to the light and hold them against me. It was like he viewed me as things I had done in my past, and I was constantly trying to prove myself to him. He never forgave me for aborting our child; he viewed me as a selfish murderer. He would say that I used to smoke pot, cigarettes party, and took interest in same sex relations—and he would always bring those things up. "What kind of trainer are you, you used to smoke? You drink all the time, you are a fake." "Those clients are not your friends. They do not like you. They act like they do because they pay you for a service." It felt like the moment I started regaining my confidence back, he began to slowly start to break me down. It may have been a subconscious thing he was doing without realizing it. After all, I did get high and mighty before and just up and divorced him once before.

The more and more I heard these things, the more and more I believed them and became them. I became more and more depressed. I did not go out, and I was isolated with what I was being told about myself. The work hours that Jack had were causing so much stress on him, and I was not making things any easier at home, always raising my complaints. He was working nights and sleeping days. He was working sometimes eighty hours a week. I was trying to get some hours in, but it was constantly conflicting with his schedule. His patience would run out a lot of times, and the way he'd get his point across was to raise his voice.

The stressful situation would cause Jack to yell at Chloe, and I knew it was wrong, but I did not know how to show him he was wrong. He did not have a loving home or good parents, so he did not know how to discipline other than with an iron fist. Chloe had a snow globe collection she had in her room. She was very proud of it. She had snow globes from different times of the year and from different parts of the country. Chloe also had a habit of breaking things around the house just as any kid would. She somehow broke the remote control, and Jack had just paid to replace it. When he heard she had dropped it and it broke, he went down to her room and started smashing all of her snow globes on the floor one after another. It was like he had snapped. She was screaming at him to stop. He said to her, "Now you know how it feels to have something of yours broken. I bet now you'll never break anything in this house again." I felt nauseous. I knew he was wrong.

Chloe did not fully understand whatever lesson he was trying to show her. It was awful. I did not talk to him for days after that. He finally realized he was wrong, and he tried to make amends, so he went out and bought her piggy bank days later and told her to start a new collection of those. He really thought that would make everything okay. He just did not get it.

More and more I knew this was not the life I was intended to live. Jack was a workaholic and worked all the time, so I spent a lot of time alone away from my friends and with the kids. His schedule was all over the place making it hard for him to adjust. He was working some nights and then some days at first. We only had one car so the kids and I would walk everywhere we needed to go, to the pool or to Walgreens usually. I was hard for me to go and see Layla and Blake with only having one car also. I was seeing a counselor off and on during the years I was with Jack. He never went with me because he said I was the one with the problem. He always said if I heard it from someone else besides him, maybe I'd believe it.

I went to a Christian counselor and was told I could not be helped until I found an anchor and identity in Christ. He did also think that I was overmedicated, and questioned the diagnosis. He told me there was a battle going on for my mind. I had no idea what that meant, but it made me feel rejected. I honestly believed that yes, I was the problem. I was prescribed antidepressants, sleeping pills, and even lithium for bipolar disorder. Since I was told I was all those things, I became the labels. As you believe, so it shall be. I remember thinking, *Well, since I have these diagnoses, it's no wonder I keep messing everything up.* They became my crutch. Jack used them against me as well. The reasons why I was diagnosed these things was never looked into, the focus was all about that *I* was the diagnosis. I remember years prior working with women just like me, fighting depression and taking all kinds of medication—I was the one back then who could not understand how a person could get that way, and that would *never* me.

I continued to give all I could to my clients, but I had nothing inside to give. I put off an outward appearance that was a direct lie of what I was feeling inside. It was exhausting, faking in front of my clients and in front of a packed kickboxing class week after week. Jack would tell me what a horrible wife and mother I was. He was right, I had no reserves left for myself or my family, and it showed in my behavior at home. He constantly berated me with words, and I would give it right back. I was told I was lazy, dumb, uncleanly, a liar, a hypocrite, bad mother, lousy wife, and that I would never make it on my own. He complained that I never cooked or cleaned, and it really gave me grief when I'd tell him I was depressed but could not really explain why. He'd say, "At least, you should know why you feel something, and not just feel it." Was he right? I had no idea; I was just so worn down and unhappy and hurting. The worst was when he told me it was his fault that he married a crazy bitch just like his mother. So now I was asking him, "Am I really that bad?"

GOD, IS THAT YOU?

The only thing I could do at this point was start running. So I did—I literally started running. I ran every day, pushing Olivia in the jogger stroller, with the dog. I started a running group, and we did races together. I was feeling better. Running did help me to cope with the pain. Eventually, I realized I was running from something, but getting nowhere. I got up to running about fifty miles a week. I then would attach my self-worth to the amount of miles I'd run or did not run. I'd listen to the gospel CD I got years ago while I ran; I'd hear the words, and they would give me power. I would run right past Grace Church almost every day, and I would say to myself, "I need to go there one day." Grace is a huge campus that sits on a hill. I'd force myself to run right up that hill without stopping. There is a huge cross at the top of the hill I would just marvel at every time I got to the top. At that time, I did not know how marvelous the cross was and what it would mean for me.

One Sunday, I got the girls ready and we went to Grace Church. We liked it, so we went again. It was as if the preacher was speaking directly to me the entire time! The words he was saying were piercing right to my heart. I'd been to church growing up all my life, but never truly grasped anything worthwhile from it; this completely got my attention. The pastor knew my struggle. He was telling me it was never meant for me to live like this. They showed a clip on a big screen of a runner with this shackle on his wrist. He would start to run, and then he would be pulled back down, then he would start to run again. The same thing would happen over and over again. Then he looks up to God, and the shackle was removed, and he was able to run again. It clicked for me then! I was *not* my past mistakes. I was so excited about this revelation. At the end of service, the pastor invited anyone who felt like they needed to make a change in their life but wanted help from the Holy Spirit to break the chains that held them to stand up. I stood up. I was one of those people. This is a huge congregation, and there were many people there, but I stood up. He then said, "If you are a believer and you near someone who is standing, place your hands somewhere on the person who is standing, and we will pray for them." I was amazed at all the people around me who placed their hands on me and prayed for me. I felt like I broke free from all the chains right there. After the prayer, I got several hugs and words of encouragement from complete strangers; it was like they knew where I was. I felt alive. Something was different. There was hope for me, and I just knew it. I went home. Jack was asleep since he worked nights.

I decided to barbeque, so I sat outside, and God began to show me that I was forgiven of everything I ever did wrong in my past. I was sitting there in front of the fire. I remember it was really humid outside, but I could also feel the warmth of God's love. I was rocking back and forth, speaking out loud to God, asking him to forgive me for everything I'd ever done. I laid my heart opened to him, and everything that I ever felt guilty about came flooding to my mind and out of my mouth. It would come to my mind, I would just say it, and then it was like it was then deleted somehow. Right then and there, I put down all my baggage forever and found rest in his arms. I understood that Jesus died in my place, to give me his righteousness. He took on what I deserved, but since I received his gift of righteousness, I was now free.

A huge weight was lifted, and I was free—free indeed. I wanted Jack to wake up, so I could share this joy with him. I knew if it was for me, it was for him to feel this way too. He did wake up that afternoon, and I ran to him and gave him a huge hug right away. I told him that I am forgiven, and I am not what my past says. I am that I have a brand new start in Christ. Then he says the strangest thing: he says "Yes, I've been telling you that." What? No, he had not ever, but I kept on talking about it. He then said, "Well, I don't want to 'steal your joy'" (his words exactly, very poignant). I'm going to go in the other room and watch TV. He was not enthused at all; in fact, I thought he was suspicious. I was still on top of the world, and his response did not ruin my day.

As soon as I stepped into agreement with God, the enemy reared its head and worked hard to get me back down where I was. Jack came at me more and more now. He told me he knew I was cheating with another man and to just tell him instead of keeping him in the dark about it. I told him the new man is *Jesus*. I was serious. He looked at me and told me I was crazy.

One of my mom's sister's had passed a month before, and she left me with an unexpected fifteen hundred dollars (she also had complications with scleroderma, same as my grandpa). That extra money afforded us to get a second car. We got the car, and so now I had a little more freedom. Jack began tracking my phone, checking my text messages. I did not know this until he called me one day and asked me where I was. I told him the truth, and he said I was lying because my phone said I was somewhere else. He had just gotten a new smart phone that he did not fully know how to work, so I am sure his coordinates were off. He had called the center, and I was not there. I told him I was not at the center, that I was leaving city hall. I had a group of women I trained on their lunch break over there. He knew this.

So that night I got home, he had made a sandwich for his lunch to take to work, and he sat it on the counter. I took the kids to the Laundromat because the dryer quit working. When we got back, he started questioning me about his sandwich. He asked me if I ate it and went on and on, and I said no. What was he talking about? He was already loopy because of his work schedule. It dawns on him that it was probably the dog, so he closed in on her. He yells at her, "Yeah, bitch! I know you ate it" He pulls the dog up by her collar, so she was standing on her hind legs and starts punching the dog in her ribs. She is howling, and the girls are crying for their daddy to stop. I was stunned, and I froze. What was happening? Jake had never been physical like that. He was always verbal, even in discipline with the kids. He never even spanked our kids.

He then came at me, saying that it was my fault and I should have never gotten the dog in the first place. He grabs my arm and pulls me down the hallway, and then tells me to read his lips because I am stupid and I might miss what he is trying to tell me. He pulled me down on the couch and says, "Get rid of that dog, or I will do it for you. What stupid person adopts a dog and two cats in the same week? My stupid wife, that's who!" By this time, I was bawling. The kids were upset and scared also. Then he left for work.

This was not right, something was definitely different. I knew Jack was under a lot of stress with bills and sleep deprivation, but this was not good. I got the kids to settle down and got them to bed. I talked to Ellen, my boss on the phone, and then I called my mother—no one had any real advice for me. There were no answers; the devil had indeed stolen my joy just that quickly. Satan had a stronghold and fed off my fear, doubt, and shame, and dragged me right back down where I was before. The spiritual battle for my soul had intensified.

I drew a really hot bath, grabbed a cold beer, and got in the tub. I was numb, and I had been in this place several times before—a place of defeat, a place where I did not care to fight anymore, a place where nothing I did mattered anymore, and no one could help me. All of Jack's words started swirling in my head: "You are stupid. You are a fake. You are lazy. You are a lousy wife. You are a liar. You are a murderer, and you are just like my mother. A fifteen-year-old could take better care of our kids than you." On and on, his words swirled around in my head as I lined up all the pills I was going to take. I had plenty of Zoloft, Ambien and lithium. I was ready to end my life right then and there; I had all the medication I needed to take and some beer to wash it down with. I said to myself, "He is pushing me to kill myself, just like his other wife. If that is what he wants, that is what he will get."

Just as I settled into that thought, I heard a still small voice: "Flee this place. I have plans for you." Amongst all the noise in my head, I heard those words as clear as a bell. I immediately got out of the tub and started packing things. I was not sure where I was going, or when, but I got some of my stuff and some of the kid's stuff. I was not sure what I was doing, but I was sure I had to obey that voice. I prayed that night. I said, "If this is you, God, show me the way to go. Help my precious babies and me."

The next morning, I got the kids ready, and I went to work as usual. Olivia was at the day program at the center, and Chloe went to day camp at the park. I had some of our stuff in the trunk; I put it there the night before. I had no clue what came next. When I got to work, I told a coworker what happened the night before, and she told me to go and file a restraining order. She said that the physical abuse of an animal was a definite sign of anger escalating and that I or one of the kids could be next. Was it that serious? *Yes.* So I did what she said and went down to the courthouse. I turned my phone off so he could not track me. I got the restraining order, got back to work, and turned my phone on.

I had about six missed calls from Jack. I was really nervous and shaking. I called him back, and he immediately wanted to know where I was then. He then said he was at the store, looking at dryers, and wanted to know what kind I wanted. What? He thought everything was just fine after what happened the night before? Then he asked what I was doing. I told him I was at work. I got off the phone and turned it off. I went in to work, and my coworkers rallied around me. I told them I could not go back. One of Olivia's teachers said her and her family were leaving town for fourteen days and that I could stay at her house, but not until Monday. God brought everything I needed right on time. I left work and went to the bank and got out what money I had saved for the kids' Christmas, about four hundred dollars. I went and I got a new phone in my own name. It had officially begun my journey to find whole peace, God's way. It started with hearing, and then obeying the voice of my Father in heaven. He was calling me out of darkness and making a way for me.

Grandpa Jones With Blake 1992 Memorial Day

Grandpa Jones with Layla 1994

My mother and I 2 days before Blake was born 1991

Me and Baby Blake

Me and Baby Layla and Blake 1993

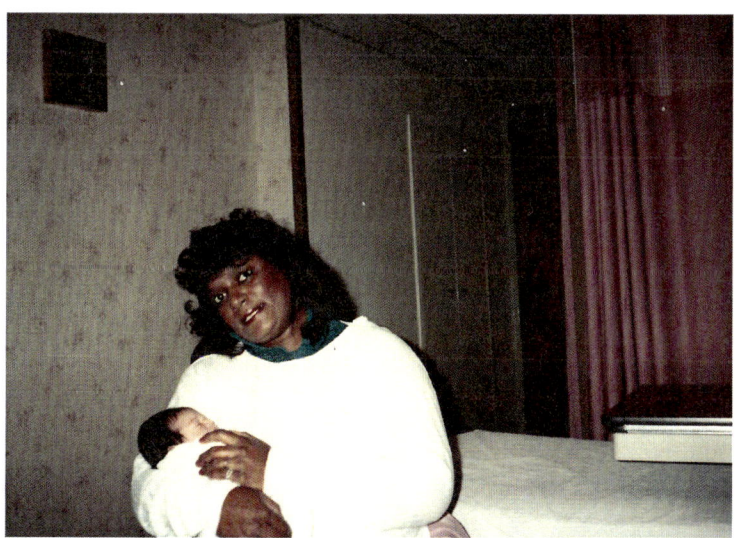

Mom with Baby Layla

Mom with Blake and Layla going to church

Blake and Layla after our trip to Disney

Blake and Layla

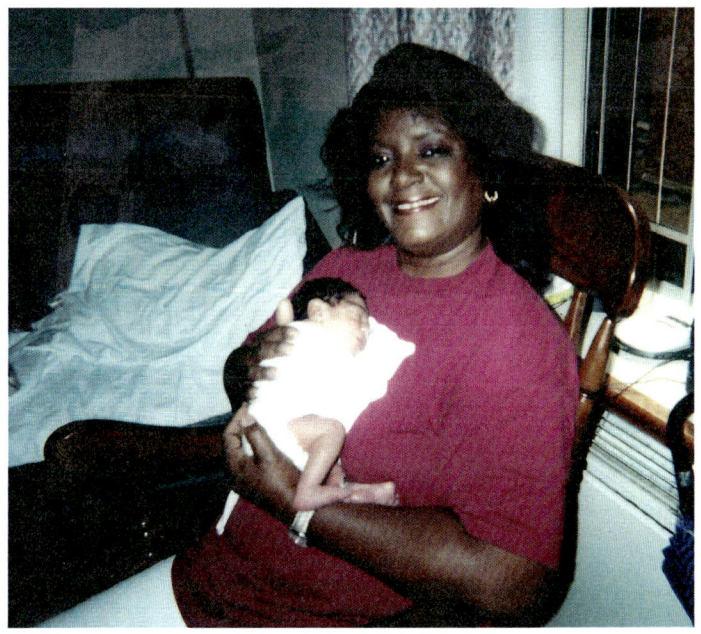

Mom with Baby Chloe

Me giving baby Chloe a bath in the sink

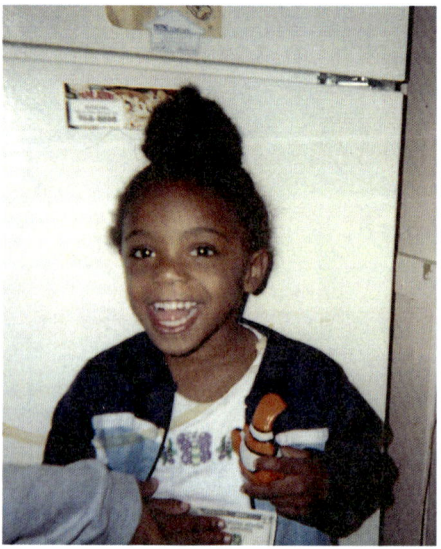

Chloe as a toddler

Chloe in 2008

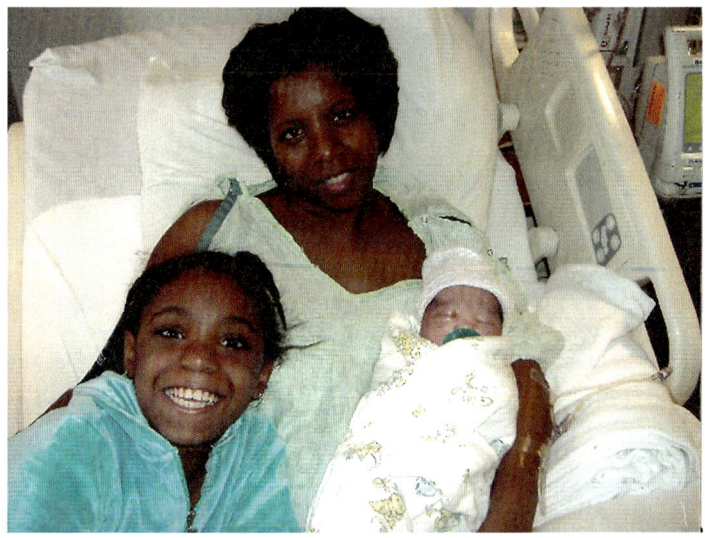
Me with Chloe and new baby Olivia

Baby Olivia 2008

Me with baby Olivia on my birthday 2008

Chloe and Olivia

My dad with Olivia and Chloe

Chloe and Olivia at the pumpkin patch

Blake and Layla all grown up 2013

Me and my brother when we were younger

Me and My brother Thanksgiving 2013

Me with all the kids Christmas 2013

PART 2

*"You Are My Child.
I Will Make a Way for You"*

GOD IS WITH ME

Ever since I heard that still small voice tell me to flee that place, I began to see clearly there was a way being made for me. I had been doing life my own all wrong. Going from one situation to another, never having peace and always being left empty, all the while trying to hold it together for appearances' sake. So broken inside and I could not fix it, I needed a savior. For months, I tried to save money and plan a way that I could leave the situation I was in. God stepped in and said it was time to move, so I moved. God made the way out of no way. I obeyed his call, and it changed my life forever.

That night, I took the girls over to my friend Jessica's house. She and her husband, Rick, said we could stay there for the weekend. Rick was the chiropractor I had been seeing for my back issues, after all the running I was doing. His wife, Jessica, worked in the office alongside him. That night, I was running on pure adrenaline, and everything was just falling into place. Jack knew that I had become friends with Rick and Jessica just a few months prior when I started going to their office for adjustments and therapy. God's provision once again—placing godly people in my life whom I could reach out to.

Even though I had not known Jessica for very long, we had an immediate (divine) connection. We got along instantly, and we talked about everything. I started training her on a regular basis, so we became really good friends. She had experienced an encounter I had with Jack first hand, just weeks prior. She went with me as a guest to my friend Valerie's birthday dinner. Valerie is an old girlfriend of my brother's, whom I'd known for a long time. Her and my brother did not end up together, but she and I remained friends. She knew Jack and was one of the few people he approved of me hanging out with from time to time. Every year, Valerie had a party for her birthday. This year, I did not want to tell Jack I was going to the birthday dinner because I just knew it would lead to an argument. I had planned on taking the kids to Jessica's house and have her teenage daughter watch them while her husband, John, was at home also. Jessica and Rick have a little girl the same age as my Olivia, and a son close to the age of Chloe, so they all enjoyed playing together. I knew the kids would be fine—there was no doubt in my mind about it. I could only be gone a couple hours since I needed to pick Jack up from work that night at about 10 p.m.

We got to the restaurant, found the birthday party, and decided where we were going to sit. As soon as we put our order in for food, Jack called me on my phone to ask where I was, even though he already knew this as he had been tracking my phone.

I told him, and he immediately started yelling at me and told me to get up and leave right then and there. He was really mad that I had left the girls with people he did not personally know. I reminded him that he had met the Doctor and his wife, and they were good people. Olivia got along well with their daughter, and the kids were fine. They were being watched by their teenage daughter, and the Dr. Rick was at home. He told me that I had poor judgment of people, and I needed to clear things with him before making plans like that without telling him. I told Jessica we had to leave. She looked at me and said very calmly, "We just got here. We are going to stay. Tell him the kids are fine, and you will be there to pick him up." I could not tell him that. Something in me felt like he was right and I was wrong. Jessica could see that I was uncomfortable with that decision, so we soon got up and left.

On the drive home, Jessica talked to Jack on the phone to try and calm him down. She now worried for my safety. Needless to say, he did not say anything nice to her. She told me right then and there that he was way out of line and that behavior was uncalled for. She said that he was abusive in his language, and no one should ever be treated that. Was she right? Did I deserve that? After all, she did not know every detail of my past. I did deserve the life I have, didn't I? The next day, Jack shut off my cell phone and told me that since I put my friends before him, and that I text everyone else more than I text him, that I did not need a phone. That just showed me that I was indeed being treated like a child, and I did not deserve that. The cell phones as well as all the bills were in his name, so there was nothing I could do.

When the girls and I got to their house that night, I explained to them that Daddy was very angry, and we could not be around him when he was like that. They completely understood. They were scared that he would hurt me. They did see how he beat the dog and how he grabbed me just the other night. I did go back over to the house with a police officer later that same night since I knew he would be at work. I needed to get more of our stuff and also get the dog. I went to the police department. I had called Gina on the drive over; she kept me calm. She worked in the police department, so she told me exactly what I needed to do. I got there and asked for a police escort to go over to house with me.

An officer followed me over to the house. I was relieved Jack's car was indeed gone, so he was not there. We got into the house, and I grabbed as much as I could. My heart was racing. Going back into that house again made my skin crawl. It was cold and dark in there. The officer who was with me was the same officer who responded to the call just a year earlier when Jack's wife had died. That was sort of eerie. The officer told me the house felt the exact same way it did when he was there the last time. He made a comment to me that kind of stung. He said the other wife committed suicide and "you still went back to that man?" Yes, I sure did. I left my old cell phone by the door as I left. That way, he would know it was done, and that I had been there.

I had it arranged to meet a coworker and former client to keep the dog for the weekend. She loved animals and was more than willing to help me out. I met her and her boyfriend late that night, and they took the dog. I made it back to Jess and Rick's house and got the girls to bed. The weekend with them there was really nice. I could breathe a sigh of relief; I did not worry about what was to come next. It was as if the plan would be shown to me as I went along. That weekend, we enjoyed great food and great company. The girls got to play with the Wii game system, and their house was gorgeous. We slept on the pullout couch downstairs; we were safe.

After the weekend was over, we went to stay at the house of Olivia's teacher, Monica. Her family was leaving town for two weeks, and we were welcomed to stay in their home. That was a huge blessing, and I was so thankful. Their house was close to our old house, so I was nervous that we would run into Jack. I took the girls to day camp as usual since I still had to work. I got a page on the overhead system from one of the teachers. It said for me to come to the preschool area where Olivia was. She said Jack had called and was on hold for her to find out if I was in the building. I told her to stall him while I called the police and had a police officer come up to the center while I got Olivia and was able to leave. I was an employee, and I worked in the same building where Olivia went to preschool. God's provision once again.

I had let my friends on Facebook know what was going on in my life. The outpour of support was huge. People gave us clothing, food, money, and gift cards. We had offers from people who had furniture to give us, and other people wanting to help us move. Someone even gave us a huge bag of dog food and treats for our dog. God's blessings were all around us. This showed me that yes, I was dearly loved and I had indeed touched other's lives along the way. All those years I was told the opposite, and I believed the lies! I knew I was on the right path. The ladies I trained at city hall gave me a gift card, and so I went to the store and bought a beautiful cross necklace that had the serenity prayer on it: "Give me the serenity to accept the things I cannot change, and the courage to change the things I can and the wisdom to know the difference."

I was very serious about filing for a divorce from Jack. That was the next step in my mind. I felt like God never ordained our marriage in the first place, so I would not offend God if I filed. Gina, a client of mine, recommended a good lawyer whom a friend of hers had used. I went to see this lawyer, who was rather pricey but very good at what he did. I told him I was a personal trainer, and if he needed a trainer, I would work some of the bill off by doing a trade. He told me his daughter was a trainer, and it ended up that I knew the woman she worked for. He then dropped his five thousand-dollar retaining fee, and he told me to get three hundred dollars in the office the next day, and he would go ahead and file that day (*God's grace*). He said that it would be best if I filed first, and that it was better to start with the ball at the top of the hill rather than at the bottom. He told me that I did not need to let Jack see the girls since I was very afraid of what he might do at the time. He also advised me to get a full-time job. He said that I was an attractive, able bodied person, and the judge would show favor if I was gainfully employed. It was nice to hear that. I had been limited to the hours I could work for so long under the regime of Jack.

This was a remarkable group of women whom I trained at the city hall building on their lunch break. These women were all blessings sent as God's provision for me once again; I just never realized it. The workout group started out very large with about fifteen people. We would work out all together in the municipal courtroom. This group did size down to six faithful women. These women left in the group were each a blessing to me in their own special way. I worked with Josie, a very caring woman who worked out very hard in the gym. She always took time to listen to me, without judgment, anytime I needed to talk. Trina worked in the finance department. She was in the best shape among everyone, but she still would help everyone in the group stay motivated. Virginia worked in the IT department. These women were so dedicated that when Jack's work hours switched, and I did not have a car during the workout times, Virginia would come and pick me up and then take me back home after our workout sessions. I would also have to bring Olivia with me when I trained these women. There was a time when Jack did not want Olivia to be in day care. They did not care; they just wanted me as their trainer. Terri worked in the police department and was the organizer of the group. She would make sure we had the right equipment we needed available to us in the gym. Claire worked in planning. She was the comic of the group and kept everyone laughing with her one-liners and sarcasm, same as with Gina who was formerly worked in the police department but now worked customer service. God armed me with these women who could really help me, but at the time I had no idea. These women rallied around me like no other.

After meeting with the lawyer, I asked the workout group if they could pay me a month in advance so I could gather the funds to pay for the attorney. They all paid in advance and gave some extra without even batting an eye! I was blown away. God was pouring out his grace, love, and affection to me through these women. I went back the next day and gave the attorney the three hundred in cash. It was then I had filed for divorce, and there was no turning back.

During the time we stayed at Monica's house, I once again called the Christian counselor I saw the one time. I told him that I understood what he was trying to tell me so many months earlier. I had found my anchor and hope in God. God was all I had now, and he was showing his love for me in many ways. I started seeing the counselor again every week, as well as going to church. I was starting to find out who I was made to be. I started to renew my mind with God's truth. The counselor would listen to me and show me passages of scripture about who God wanted me to be, and how he waits for us to return to him so he can give us life more abundantly. He would also pray for me and ask the Lord's blessing for me after each session. This man was anointed, and I was so thankful God brought him to me.

I got a call from Josie. She asked if I saw the internal posting about the customer service job at city hall. I told her I knew nothing about it. She said to me, "Get your resume together and send it over there. You need a full-time job with benefits, and this could be the job for you." I did not hesitate (God's timing).

I started working on my resume, and in doing so, I was sort of discouraged because all of my experience was mostly fitness sales and management. I had some great accomplishments in those areas. I knew that I could get along with people because I knew how to treat them, and I also had a great attitude. Josie had told me they were having a hard time finding a third person for the customer team. They had just gone through two people they hired in a very short time. Josie told me she did not know what the problem was since it was not her department, but she was sure things would be different with me in the position. She had confidence in me. Just hearing her say that to me gave me confidence that I could indeed do the job. The power of words once again.

A couple of months prior, I was able to make more money by picking up some hours at the center working the front desk. During that time, I learned the phone system and how to use the computer. That gave me some confidence because of the fact that I was able to learn something so quickly.

I got a call for an interview for the job at city hall. I was happy but very nervous about it. I did not have full confidence that I would get the job. I believed in God for sure now, and I prayed more, but I still had doubts that he really had my back and that I was redeemed of my past failures. My mind was not fully renewed, and my faith was small at this point. The interview was very intense. I went into the interview a little nervous. It seemed to me the line of questioning was somewhat attacking. I was asked to explain why I would be good for the position. I was also asked a lot of questions regarding conflict resolution. I kind of felt somewhat ambushed. I really could not image what I would do in some of the scenarios that were being described. I answered the questions as best I could. I then had a short interview with the person in charge of the department. I basically told her that I could do any job I was trained to do since I had an infectious personality and good attitude. She agreed that a good attitude was not something one could just learn. I felt like I did okay with that part of the interview. I did not feel like I had the job when I left. It was not in my hands.

GOD IS IN CONTROL

Meanwhile, I was trying to figure out where we were going to live after the two weeks at Monica's were up. I had been given numbers to different shelters and none were taking new residents, so mom went with me to look for an apartment. I had little to no credit, so I was hoping she would cosign for a place for me to stay. Since I did not have a full-time job, she was a little worried about doing that, but she was there to help. We looked for something I could afford, and yet we came up empty. I was starting to feel defeated and not sure what I was going to do next. It almost felt like it was a sign to give up and stop trying. We had been looking for an apartment for me all day, and when we pulled up in the driveway of Monica's house, I got a call from my brother. He said that I needed to call Angel, that she was trying to get a hold of me and that she had a place I would be able to stay for free (God's grace).; I did not hesitate. I called her. Angel was my mentor when I worked with at the women's gym. She now lived in Las Vegas, running her own business in women's figure training. She said she had a high school friend who had a mother who had a huge home and was hoping to get someone in it with her to help her keep it clean and keep her company. So basically, I could move in with the girls and just clean. Yep, I can do that. She told me the woman lived in O'Fallon, and she would call me back with more details. Thank you, Lord. I really could see his hand in all of this. He was opening every door as I went along.

The girls and I went out to the house on Sunnyview Lane. It was indeed a multimillion dollar home. It was beautiful from the outside but needed some work on the inside. We met Brenda. She was very sweet, and the girls grew to call her Grandma Bren. She was a widow and Kristen was her only daughter. Kristen was the one who was friends with my mentor, Angel. She welcomed us right away. She showed us the rooms we could stay in. Brenda had two huge German Shepherd dogs. They were sweet as can be, and our dog made herself right at home with them.

I was given the master bedroom on the main floor. It had its own bathroom with a huge jet-powered tub and a standalone shower with multiple showerheads. There was a huge vanity mirror and double sinks. There was a small laundry room in the room also. There was a front-loading washer and dryer in it with a built-in ironing board in the wall. The closet was huge, with an entire wall dedicated for shoes. Olivia had the room across the hall from me. It was already decorated for a little girl, and it had its own full bathroom also. Chloe had a room that was upstairs. She had her own bathroom also. Needless to say, the girls were thrilled. There was a pool in the backyard and a trampoline and a play set.

Josie and Terri came over that weekend and helped me clean out and bag up Kristen's things. She had lived there with Brenda and just recently moved out. She had a lot of stuff, to say the least. Terri was superb at organizing, and Josie was very helpful with the cleaning. I was able to get things all set up with their help. Those girls were amazing, and a huge help to me.

Kristen took the kids out to the mall and bought some new clothes for them. Chloe was so excited to show me all the great stuff she got. Kristen also told her friends I was in need, and they donated all kinds of items to the girls and me. She was able to get a bed for me and a brand new comforter and sheet sets for the girls. She would make trips over to the house to bring more and more stuff for us every time she'd return. She had friends who donated bags and bags of clothing and shoes and household items. God was showing us his love. These strangers did more for me at this time of my life than my own family did.

I got Chloe enrolled at the school. Brenda had to go with me up to the school to sign an affidavit that I was living at the house with her. I was able to get Chloe's IEP set up right away, and things were going nicely. The teachers and counselors at the school were very helpful. She would be starting sixth grade at the middle school. Kristen made sure she had all her school supplies. She got her backpack, pens, paper, and everything. Chloe was very excited. I applied for foods stamps. I was working part time at the center, which was only about $13,000 a year.

Things were going well with the move in. The kids were acclimating well to the new surroundings. They were starting to miss their dad though. I had contacted his sister, Mary, to let her know to tell Jack the kids were fine. She did talk to the girls on the phone, so she knew for herself they were doing okay. I always liked Jack's sister, Mary. She was a true Christian woman who walked closely with the Lord, and it showed in everything she did. She loved kids and would always do things for all my kids. She never hesitated to babysit or even loan me her car on occasion whenever my work schedule at the center would conflict with Jack's. I eventually called Jack, so now he had my new phone number. He began to call often and leave horrible voicemails. His moods and attitudes would fluctuate; it was very strange. Sometimes he would talk about how sorry he was, and then other times he would use threatening language.

The odd thing was that he reached out to my mother, of all people. He talked to her quite often after we left. She was his sounding board. She would let me know that he was not ready to see the girls. She could tell his behavior was not very consistent. She was right. One night, I had my brother's SUV at the house while my brother had my car. My brother just got this vehicle, so it was not one Jack would have been familiar with. Jack left an angry voice mail saying something about my having someone sleeping over at the house with the girls there. He saw a car that he did not know, so he assumed that it was someone spending the night with me. He still had it in his head that I was with someone else. That only told me he knew where I was now living.

The next day when I was gone, Brenda said Jack came out to the house, and she called the police to have him removed. She said he started off calm, and then he ended up trying to be forceful with his language. Brenda told me not to be surprised if he tried to retaliate with an order to get the kids back from me. She was right. My lawyer's office called, saying there was paperwork for custody of the kids. He had stated that I was mentally ill and off of my medication and the kids were in danger being with me. So it had begun—the spiritual battle. The enemy wanted me to be afraid because of my past mistakes and take on worry, shame, and blame for all of this. Since my faith was still quite small, it was a struggle for my mind to comprehend that God was on my side—that he knew my heart and that he was in control, and none of the enemy's tricks would work.

A week later, I got another call to come back to take a clerical test for the job. That just had to mean that they liked me enough to take the time to test me. I felt like there was hope for me. I did awful at the test. I knew nothing about using word documents or formatting letters. I could not type fast either. I just knew that was the end of that. I had really lost all confidence after I took that test. The girls at my lunchtime workout group built my confidence back up by telling me that test was very ancient, and it would not really count for much. They told me not to worry about it. So I didn't. I had a good reputation in the city because of my work history at the center. It was all the same municipality. The women I knew who worked at city hall had nothing but good things to say about me.

The next week, I was called in for another interview. This time, it was with the customer service team I would be working with if I got hired. The other girls who worked customer service were Mindy and Gina. I already knew Gina since she was a client of mine. Mindy I only knew of by seeing her at the front desk when I came over to train the lunchtime workout group. The interview was exhausting. I was already under so much stress with all the current changes in my life. There were the same types of questions from before. Questions like: "What would you do if you were scheduled to go to lunch and a team member told you, you would have to go a different time without explanation of why." I was not sure what kind of answer they were looking for. I was kind of naive in the business world. I asked at the time, "Why would anyone want to cause a problem with that for no reason?" I was guessing that the job I was applying for had some issues that may come along with it. That interview lasted for two hours. I was exhausted when I left, and once again, I was not at all sure I had done any good in that interview.

A few days went by, and I still had not heard anything about the job. I was sort of worried, but not really. I had a kind of a peace about it. I was on the right track with everything, so if this was the path I was to take, I would soon know. I was getting along with Brenda, and the kids were doing well. I found out fast that I would be doing a lot of cleaning at the house. Kristen had three kids that would come over and stay with us after school. Her kids were sweet-natured and well-behaved—but they were kids, and kids make messes. So between her three kids and my two kids and the three dogs, and a huge house with lots of things to pull out, I was constantly picking up after someone or another. I'd help with keeping the kitchen clean, and with the dishes, and with keeping the front room clean. I also cleaned three bathrooms.

Then I got the call. They wanted to offer me the position with the customer service team. I was so excited I got the job; I was being given an opportunity. I would have full-time pay with great benefits. I would be a full-time municipal employee. There was no doubt in my mind that God's hand was reaching out to me, saying, "I will help you, just trust and obey me." I went in to sign my acceptance letter. It was explained that I was being hired on a two-week probationary period. They would see how I adjusted to the team and how well I was able to pick up on the training. Then at that time I would be put on thirty-day probation, and then fully hired after sixty days. I did not care what hoops I had to jump through; I knew I had the power of the Holy Spirit living in me, and I would be okay.

I started working at city hall. I would have a longer commute to and from work than I was used to. I had to be at work at 8:30 a.m., and Olivia's morning program began at 9 a.m. I called and asked Monica if she could help me out. She agreed that I could drop Olivia off at her house in the mornings, and she would drive her to school with her. Monica was one of the teachers at the community center. I was glad that would work out.

I started my on-the-job training with Gina. She had only been in the customer service position almost a year now. It was a very strange dynamic because I was her fitness trainer in the gym, and now I had a submissive role to her by having her train me on information that I did not know. What made it even more challenging was that I was still doing her workouts in the group on our lunch break, downstairs in the gym. We would literally reverse our roles at lunch time, where I would tell her what to do, and then we would return back to work afterwards to have her train me the rest of the day. That was so strange for me. At times, I could not humble myself in front of her while I was learning something I did not know. I felt like I should know everything. That alone became exhausting mentally. I did not work as closely with Mindy, so I did not know her as well, and I knew Gina. Our personalities did not quite mix well. Mindy was exceptional at her job and had been doing it for a very long time. Here I was—this person with very little experience joining a team that she was very territorial over. There were times when we would be together at the desk if Gina was off. I would share with her the types of things I was going through in my divorce. There were times we could talk, and then other times we just could not even deal with each other. Our moods would clash kind of like sisters at times. It was a very strange thing.

The fact that I now worked a full eight-hour day confined to a desk in dress clothes was another whole set of differences for me, then add in the forty-five-minute commute home, and then coming home to a messy house that was not mine. I was used to wearing tennis shoes and workout clothes all day and having a flexible workday. The stress was starting to mount. I would begin to have a drink every night and take a hot bubble bath to relieve the stress, as I also was now battling acne and some minor back pain.

I was going to church, but my faith was very weak. I was renewing my mind with the word of God; it was still mostly in my head and had not fully made it down to my heart.

During this time, I did talk to Jack on the phone, and whenever he would begin to talk to me in an unwelcome manner, I would simply hang up on him. I remember him telling me that he was going to arrange the visitation schedule, and I needed to tell my lawyer to back off. That conversation ended with the end call button right away. It was back and forth like that all the time. He was going to try to control everything along the way. I did not fully see this at this time, but it was already beginning. He did seem impressed that I was able to get a full-time job. I remember him telling me that was all I ever really ever needed to do in our marriage before—to help with the bills. What? That was not how I remembered things.

My lawyer had advised me that I could let the girls be with their dad for a weekend. They had not seen their dad in almost thirty days. I was scared to death he would not return them to me, but he did. I had to remember that he was not used to having the kids for very long all by himself. I was definitely the primary caregiver for the girls. We would have to wait until we had an actual visitation schedule in place by the judge. A hearing for that was not scheduled. We still had appearances for the restraining order and also his counter to that. As the weeks went on, he seemed to become easier to deal with. I began to drop my guard some. He said he went to his lawyer and dropped whatever he had against me, and then we had missed the court date for the restraining order also.

RESHAPING AND MOLDING BEGINS

I remember Brenda and Kristen warning me about not going back, that was the farthest thing from my mind. I did notice that the more and more I talked to Jack, the more he would try to gain control. He kept saying that we needed to fire our lawyers and work this on our terms. That did make sense to me. He told me he dropped the paperwork he had filed, and he also said that he read all of the journals I left at the house. I had forgotten to get them. That really hit me hard. It made my stomach turn over to think about the fact that he read through all of my private journals, and then he gave them to his lawyer to read (very ironic as I am writing this tell-all book). But at that time, I did not fully realize that all I had done was not who I was. He said he gave them to the lawyer since it mapped out my planning to leave the relationship. I thought to myself, *If anything my journals would show all the mental duress I was under for all these years.* He said he would get my journals back. I took that as a peace offering, so I began to let my guard down.

Meanwhile at my new job, I was experiencing some turbulence. I felt like I needed to learn all I needed to know, and somehow I was not getting that. We were at the two-week mark, and so I received a review. My review was not as good as I would have liked it to be. I felt like everyone was making it hard for me for some reason. I harbored a little bit of resentment. I was given an honest review, but I just did not feel like it was as good as I felt I was doing. My strengths were not in data entry and paying attention to small details in recording information. My strengths were in helping people. I started to see that this was not going to be as easy for me after all. I still used my credentials as being a personal trainer. I had my identity in that job title, even though I was working a new job now. People knew I was a trainer, and since I worked the front desk, I was always asked random fitness questions from other people who worked in the building that made me feel important for some reason.

The front desk job at city hall was not an easy job. The job was a one-person job that involved good multi-tasking skills I would soon learn. I would answer phone calls ranging from "Dead animals in the street" to "My streetlight is out" or "My sewer line is broken." Whatever problem a person had, it seemed we were the first place they would call. I helped people who came in with questions as well. I dealt with contractors and homeowners applying for and picking up permits. I collected applications and payments, entered applications, and made sure they got to the right departments. We accepted all incoming packages for the building as well so we would have to notify recipients. There was always something going on at the desk. The front desk person is essentially the gatekeeper to the building, and to the city for that matter. I felt honored being a black female to have that position. Little did I know that God was shaping and restoring my character in this new job—I just had no idea at the time.

There was talk about other positions opening in the police department. I started thinking maybe that was the way I should go. There were a few people who shared with me their experiences at the desk, and how they could not wait to get into another position. I was learning that the font desk was a good place to start, but you did not want to stay there long term.

I had talked with Terri, the other client of mine who worked directly with the police department. She said she would love to have me work with her in the PD. So I started looking forward to doing something else already before I really got settled into the position I already had. I was all over the place mentally. I was trying to plan things and jump ahead of where I needed to be. I was only allowed to be trained to a certain point since I was on a trial basis. I did not know this at the time, so I felt like everyone was holding back on me. I also battled in my own mind Gina's perception of me. I did not want to appear inferior in her eyes. After all, the capacity she knew me in was personal trainer, fitness professional. Now I was the new employee—clueless and vulnerable. God was telling me to be still and wait on him. He was ready to mold me into something great. I just had to let go of all the insecurities, worries, and doubts. I had to give in to his will. He has to humble us so he can rebuild and restore us from the inside out.

The other dynamic that played into all of this was the fact that the customer service team was a three-person team. That is always hard to keep balanced. If I seemed too cozy with Gina, it seemed to bother Mindy, and when Mindy and Gina seemed too cozy, I would feel like the outsider. These two women had been doing a three-person job with just the two of them for months, so they had a rhythm of how to do things without me. I guess I felt pressure with that. I began to cause rifts between the two of them. Whenever either of them would blow off steam about the other, somehow I'd make sure it would get back to other and vice versa. Why was I doing that? I am not really sure; I do know I wanted the approval of both of them. God was definitely shaping me up. I was almost forty years old but still so immature in many ways.

Meanwhile, Jack and I were having civilized phone conversations, for the most part. My home life at Brenda's was still very much chaotic. There was a lot going on with all the kids and pets.

I was not used to working a "real job" forty hours a week. The commute was brutal. I just felt like there was no peace there. I was constantly cleaning, but you really could not tell. The weekends that Jack would get the kids, I had down time. That was usually the time Brenda's grandkids would be over spending time with her, so there was really no quiet down time. I would spend time with Jessica and Rick, but I would feel guilty leaving Brenda at the house when I was gone. It just seemed like I was not going to last there very long. I remember my mother telling me, "You are not going to have any peace living there." Once again, the power of her words set the tone.

During the following week, the sum pump broke in the house, and the entire house smelled of standing water. I asked Brenda how much it would cost to get it fixed, and she said it would be quite a big bill. I was working, but I still had very little money. I had gotten the washer fixed for her a few weeks before, but I really had no extra money to help out. Child support had not been set, so I was paying for Olivia's childcare, and not to mention gas to and from work. I told Jack about the situation. He went nuts. He said the kids couldn't live where there is standing water in the basement. I agreed, but I could not afford to help her get it fixed, and I could not afford to have Jack take the kids from me because of a health-hazardous living condition. I had made arrangements to move into my brother's two-bedroom apartment.

I remember getting all my clothes and things together to go stay at his house. It was dark and just being in that apartment complex parking lot, I felt immediate fear for some reason. I did not know any of the people around me. I just felt scared. I gathered my stuff from the trunk and just went into his apartment. He was out of town, so I had to get all my stuff myself. The girls were with their father. I remember trying to sleep that night on a mattress on the floor, and all I could hear was a couple yelling and fighting on the floor below. They were speaking a foreign language, but I could tell they were angry and fighting. I was trying to sleep, and I just could not do it. I got up right then and there and asked God, "What is it you want me to do? Do you want me to stay here? Where do I go God? I need you, send me a sign. Let me know what I need to do." Right then and there, I got a text from Jack. It said, "Did you make it there okay? Call me." I did not even hesitate. I called him, and I said, "I am coming home." He said okay. I replied, "I am leaving now."

MAKE MY PATH STRAIGHT, LORD

I was not sure if this was what God wanted, but I felt like it was what I needed to do. I moved back in with Jack. Chloe now would go back to her old school, and she was glad about that. The IEP we set up with the other school would follow her, so that was fine. I thought of it all as an arrangement until I was shown what I needed to do. I think Jack saw it as a chance for us to work things out. I still had it in my head that this would be temporary. That Monday at work, I told the women in my workout group that I went back to him. They all seemed to think that if that was what I needed to do, then great! The only one who actually let me know exactly what she thought was Gina. She said, "Are you crazy? Why would you ever go back to that situation after you have come so far?" I was confused about the whole thing myself, to be honest. Jack and I went to Brenda's house and got all my furniture and moved back into the same house I was told to leave just months earlier. I put all my stuff in the spare bedroom downstairs. I had all my stuff in my own room. I had a new bed that was given to me, so I would sleep in it in the spare room. Since Jack worked nights, it did not seem to matter to him. I felt like I was only staying there temporarily. We were not back together as a couple. Jack would send flowers to my job. The he started taking extra days off of work to spend time with me. It was all very sickening to me. The whole time I was there, it just did not seem right. It was as if he was forcing things, and it seemed very fake.

I now know that uncomfortable feeling of things not being right was the Holy Spirit speaking to me.

We had discussed the bills. Jack was excited to have my income of $33,000.00 coming into the household to take some of the stress off of him. He told me to just write him a check for $500.00 every two weeks when I got paid. That seemed so odd to me. It felt like a control thing. I wanted to take certain bills and just pay them directly. It rubbed me wrong, but I just ignored that feeling. It also seemed he was taking more time off work. It was weird because before he worked all the time and I could never get him to take off. He seemed to be more lax about money since I had income coming in. It seemed to me that he was putting pressure on me to stay. It was still my plan to move out of there, so I was still putting money away to make that happen. It was confusing to the kids, and it was all just wrong.

We would all go to church as a family. I was just hoping Jack would get something out of the message, but his heart was just not ready to receive it. He even started seeing the Christian counselor I was seeing. We went separately, and I was very hopeful that it would be helpful for him in some way. This was a big deal because in all our years together, he had never been to a counselor; I was the one always going trying to fix things on my own. The problem that did a arise with him seeing the counselor was that he would come back and tell me that the counselor was in agreement with him on a lot of things about me. He was now using the counselor against me somehow. I slowly started to feel defeated again, and then I remembered the spiritual battle, that the enemy will get into my head and begin to slowly break me down again if I let it happen. Every day, I was getting more and more certain that I needed to leave. We should always have 100 percent conviction if we are ever to do something. I was sure now that the move back in was to give me that absolute conviction I needed.

At work, there was tension in the threesome dynamic. I caused the rift in the team with the back and forth talk. Before long, we were all meeting with a team building consultant. This person was outsourced to help us resolve conflict within the team. I was beginning to see why all the strange questions in the interview were so important. We went over how we can use our words to communicate better. I also learned that another person's story is theirs to tell. These were all very fundamental things that I just ignored along the way. I was very immature in certain areas for my age. This new job was definitely "growing me up." I know now that God was putting me in the fire to mold me into what he needed me to be. I could not be all that he had called me to be unless I was molded into the image of his Son, which meant I had a very long way to go.

I was stressed out with my home situation, and then I had to go to work and deal with more stress. Our boss seemed very aloof to most of what was going on. I was pulled into the office on countless occasions for reprimand on not getting along with the team. I explained that I had tried on many occasions to get along. I felt like they were all out to get me, that nothing I did was ever good enough. I do know that I was good at my job. I had some clerical errors brought to my attention and often times, I would feel the need to get defensive. That was just my nature, always defending myself. Here I was doing a job that I was not made to do, but I was using my talents in people skills to do the best I could—and yet failing in the company of my coworkers. This was another form of spiritual battle, yet another way for Satan to make me feel defeated.

Our boss was a very forward thinking person, and so every time I met with her, I would have no idea of what she was ever talking about. So naturally, I only got the negative out it every time. I remember her telling me once that I was my own worst enemy. I took everything very personally, and I would get an attitude very easily with the women I worked with. I did get to help people all day, and that is something I never had a problem with. I was often told that sometimes I would go too far in helping the customer. I was told that is was not my job to answer the question but to get the caller to the right person.

I had a hard time deflecting unwanted attention from men who would come to the desk. I was hit on more than a couple times a week. Being with anyone or dating was the farthest thing from my mind. I was a wreck in need of healing, and this time I was not going to fix myself. I did not realize then that I was a certain "type" that attracted the wrong kind of attention. I was putting off an aura of weakness, so I was like prey to the wrong kind of men. I had to work on using assertive words to say in a polite way that I was not interested. Up until then, I was unable to use those words; I would just take the unwanted expressions of interest like a jab to my gut every time. God was showing me little by little my worth. Remember, I used to be the prideful girl who loved the attention of men. I was the "hot black chick with a nice rack." That girl was now being renewed at the hands of her Creator.

I had met quite a few good people working the front desk. Some would share with me their personal stories and take time to listen to what was going on in mine. I made friends with Dee; she was an inspector who took a real liking to me from the start. I told her I was looking for a place to live. She was always in the field, inspecting homes and dealing with landlords looking for tenants, so I was hopeful she could help me find a place to move to.

A few weeks after I told her I was looking for a place, she told me about a guy who rented houses and that he had one available in the area. She said she had known him and his wife for years. They were good people. Their rental homes were always clean and neat. This particular house was a zoned one-bedroom house, so they had to advertise it as such. The rent was only $575.00. The price was perfect, but I was worried and had doubts since it was a one bedroom. I really needed two bedrooms; the girls would have to share. Dee told me just to go look at it, to be sure. I went after work to go look at it. I did not tell Jack anything about this.

I found out the house was a zoned one-bedroom because the one room did not have a door on it. I had no problem using that for my room and just using a curtain. The house was 624 square feet. There was no tub, just a shower. There was no dishwasher, and no central air. There was a carport and a fenced yard for the dog. It was clean and in a safe area. The landlord wanted three months' deposit up front. I had about that much saved. The landlord told me up front the reason they would rent to me was because of Dee. She was good to them all these years, and they knew she had good judgment. I signed a lease and wrote them a check! I was so excited to have my own place. The thing I loved is that the house was in Harmony Lane. The even greater thing was that the landlord lived on a street named Delord. So literally "Delord" gave me a place to stay on "Harmony Lane." This was God and 100 percent conviction for me!

I let Jack know I got a place and I was moving out at the beginning of December. He was shocked and not very happy. He said he was hoping I would wait until he could get caught up on some bills. I told him the timing was out of my hands; this opportunity opened up just for me and I took it. We had only been moved back a little over a month. That next weekend, the girls and I moved out. Jack of course had to come and check everything out to give his approval of the house. He thought it was a safe location, and we were not too far away. He even bought us a refrigerator and moved it in. There was no doubt in my mind this was God's grace once again.

The same turbulence continued at work. I just felt like I could not do anything right. I just could not get along with the team. Was I in some way a threat to these women? I was totally the underdog for the position, so literally I had to fight every day to prove that I belonged there. There were others who showed their disapproval of me in other ways. I did my best to be nice and get along with everyone I worked with. I soon began to learn that it was not about me. People behave the way they behave, and I cannot look to myself to make them change. I could only be responsible for me. I was learning self-control. I was taking back the power I would give to people over me. This was real growth for me, only possible with God's help.

    I was beginning to grasp these truths, but the other thing that was really hard for me was seeing the women I trained during the lunch break everyday on a daily basis. Before, I would train them and then leave since I did not work there. Well now, I'd see them make trips to the snack machine and go out to lunch, instead of working out and bringing their lunch. The real problem was I was taking all of this personally. I felt invested in these women with my time, and it was as if they could care less. After all, I was working a job that was extremely difficult for me, and I was going through a divorce. I would spend my lunch breaks at work two—and sometimes three—days a week with these women, so really not ever having a break from the eight-hour day. I soon realized that I equated my self-worth with their performance. If they did well and were losing weight, I was going something right. If they did terrible, that meant it was a direct reflection of me. Here I was, working this job without a lunch break, only later to see them eat junk and drink sodas right in front of me. Wow, that was so hurtful to me because I made it about me. At the time, I did not realize that what these women did was not a reflection of me.

MY PEACE I GIVE TO YOU

We loved the little house on Harmony Lane. We were able to get every piece of furniture we needed. Kitchen table and chairs from Josie, along with a couch, a chair, and an ottoman. Gina gave us bunk beds since the girls would have to share a room. She also gave us a lot of dishes, glasses, and cups. I did not take one thing from Jack's house and that felt great. I was on my way to having whole peace. We did not have cable, and I was fine with that. I had called the cable company about cable, and they told me I would need a five hundred dollar deposit since I never have had an account with them, and that my credit was not good. Once the girls realized we would not have TV, they told their dad. He immediately jumped at the chance to help. He called and had the service put in his name. We now had cable on a twenty-inch TV. When the time came for me to pay the bill, I gave Jack a check for eighty dollars. He told me to keep my money, but he preferred a home cooked meal for maybe just dessert or me. I felt like he was being somewhat sexist, and he did give me my check back.

Jack had somehow talked me into firing my lawyer, and he had the bright idea we would use his lawyer and have something drawn up that we could both sign. He had said that we should just get a separation filed instead of getting a divorce. He said he'd hate to go through all of this again just for us to get remarried. What? Did he think this was a joke that I was getting away from him just to return again? I just wanted this whole thing over. It was already January 2012. I had filed for this divorce in

August 2011. I was already exhausted with it. But that was not even the beginning of what I would go through. I had agreed to a half and half visitation schedule without the advice of my lawyer. This schedule looked good on paper but in actuality would never work. I was agreeing to things to appease Jack. I wanted to keep him even keeled so we could get this whole thing behind us.

Layla and Blake were doing well through all of this. I would talk to them every now and then so they knew some of what I was going through. Blake had now graduated from high school. He and I were much closer than Layla and I were. My son loved me and knew I tried my best in every situation I found myself in. He always understood me and never blamed me. I remember his first heartbreak. He had a girlfriend in his senior year he really loved, and she ended the relationship before she went off to school. Blake came to visit me and we went to lunch to talk about it. He was so hurt, and there was really nothing I could do to remove this pain he was feeling. I kept letting him know that it was nothing to do with him. I explained a little bit about how I treated guys who did absolutely nothing wrong. It had been something in me that caused me to destroy relationships I was in. Somehow that was a comfort to him. He had to know that he was not the problem and not to blame himself completely for a failed relationship.

Blake had decided to move to Chicago to live with his uncle. He had planned to take some music classes and work in his uncle's pizzeria. He had a love for playing the guitar, and he was really good at it. He had only played the saxophone as a kid and had gotten an award from doing it, but never took much interest in music until *Guitar Hero* came out. He taught himself to play and read music. He had found a passion like no other, and I was so happy for him. Layla was on the honor roll at school with straight As. She played soccer, basketball, and was on the golf team. She had a new boyfriend she was spending a lot of time with now. She would come out and stay with the girls from time to time when I needed her to. Her boyfriend would come with her. Olivia and Chloe really liked him.

Jack had mentioned that working nights and seeing the girls after school was exhausting for him. He said he was going to hire a housekeeper. Right. This rubbed me wrong right from the mention of it. I remembered how things went down with "the nanny." He had placed an ad and had already been interviewing candidates from years before. I had told him that I should be a part of the process. These were our kids and that whoever he hired needed to understand they would work for both of us. It would be a way for them to have some sort of respect for me as the mother. Jack reminded me that I had a poor judgment of people and that he would just handle it. Before long, he hired Gwen. She was an older white woman from a rough part of town. I think Jack had the intention of hiring someone I knew he would not be attracted to. I happened to meet her when I was picking up the girls when I got off work. Jack was not home to introduce us properly. She came out with the kids and introduced herself, and that was fine, then she did something that appalled me right on the spot. When the kids were leaving, she bent down and hugged and kissed my youngest, right in front of me. Who did she think she was? I did not know her and was just meeting her for the first time—that was completely uncalled for. I was their mother. Here we go again. That incident pretty much set the tone for what was ahead.

I let Jack know that the girls and I would be doing a divorce care class at the church on Thursday nights. He objected to the idea because it would not be over till 8:30 p.m. at night on a school night. He was still flexing his control over everything I proposed. I could see what was happening, but it still would spend too much time worrying about things he would do, and so it still would affect my actions. I did not enroll in the class to respect his wishes. I was still trying to appease him. The weekend ahead was Super Bowl weekend, and the girls were scheduled to be with Jack. He had bragged about what a great cook Gwen was and that they were going to have a Super Bowl party at the house. I mentioned that it was a school night for the kids, and if he wanted to have a party, I could keep them. He disregarded my wishes. It would continue on like this. If I had a concern, it was disregarded, but he had the final say in everything I did. It was terrible. He was keeping the upper hand in everything. I had agreed to a certain visitation schedule without any legal advice. He worked nights the live-in housekeeper would be with the kids, and not him. This is called proxy parenting. Jack's whole purpose was to have the kids away from me and to plug someone else in, taking my place. This was the exact same thing that happened years before. He was trying to make me pay. It was a battle.

The girls were starting to struggle with everything. Olivia started wetting the bed and wanting to sleep in bed with me. She was having bad dreams and was scared, even with Chloe sleeping in the same room with her. In time, she would sleep with me and wet my bed at night. That was often very frustrating—to wake up in a warm spot of urine from my child. Chloe would begin to become more defiant with me. She would often talk back to me and be disrespectful. I would always get angry whenever I had to discipline her. I lacked good discipline skills with the kids. Jack was always the disciplinarian in the house, so now that he was not around, the kids would run me ragged. The girls would do whatever he said without question. They feared him. Sometimes I would threaten to call him just to get them to behave. I believe that since they often saw him yell and get upset with me, they now had no respect and felt they could also talk to me without respect. This was an area I needed God to help me in. I still had some insecurity that I was not a good parent, and that would be a stronghold for the devil. Since I did not have full confidence in my parenting, I had a hard time setting clear boundaries, and I would often let the girls manipulate me with the guilt of leaving their father.

I had scheduled for Chloe to spend the night with her cousins at my brother's house on the night Olivia was scheduled for a sleep study at the hospital. She had issues with snoring, and the doctor ordered the study. At first, Jack suggested Gwen go to the study and stay the night with Olivia. I completely objected to that. I was her mother, what was he thinking? When he found out Chloe was going to stay with my brother that night, he told me no. He did not like my brother and reminded me again of my poor judgment of people. He said my brother was irresponsible and that she could not go. Here he was telling me what he would except on my visitation time. Chloe was crying and upset, but I did not argue with him. I just said to myself, "God will do as he sees fit." This was not my battle. Whenever it does not make sense, it is not about you; it is a spiritual battle. When you are in Christ, he will fight it for you.

I had an appointment over at the center, so on my lunch break, I went over there. I got done with the appointment in time to go in and see Olivia at the preschool. The kids in the class were about to have lunch. The night before, Olivia had stayed the night at Jack's house. Gwen, the housekeeper, was the one to get Olivia dressed and to school. When I saw my child, it was like I got punched in the stomach. Her hair was a mess, and she had some clothes on that were too small. I could not believe what I saw. I called Jack immediately and told him it was uncalled for. The woman he hired to care for our children sent our child to school looking a mess. I could not contain myself. I took a picture of how she looked that day, in case I would need it for court purposes, and to show him what I was talking about. I went back to work in the fitness room, to my lunchtime workout group. I broke down bawling. I could hardly speak. This strange woman I did not know, and I did not hire, was in the house with my kids while their father worked nights. It seemed to me she was not doing her job well by sending them to school looking like hobos. Jack defended this woman; he said she did not know how to do black hair, and could not find any clothes that fit. I said, "So then, let me—her mother—do it I am home and able to be with my kids. Why is she there in your place during your visitation?" I called my lawyer. Apparently, he never got my letter dismissing him as my lawyer. We were able to get a PDL for visitation scheduled.

It was getting ridiculous with this woman and my children. Chloe gained ten pounds in two weeks of eating the food this woman would cook. It seemed as if she did not know what fruits and veggies were. Everything they ate was meat and starch with cream sauce and gravy. I mentioned all my concerns to Jack, but he would never pay me any mind. He would go off on me, calling me names or bringing up past behavior of mine. Whenever Jack would call the girls to tell them good night, he would ask them if they wanted to tell Gwen good night. It was as if they were a couple or something. I know his ultimate goal was to irritate and eliminate me. Any resistance I'd give him on any matter, he would retaliate with some action. Things were fine between us as long as I was going along with whatever he wanted. He had shut the cable off when he heard I called my lawyer. Since he had the service in his name, he simply called and had it shut off.

He told me to call my lawyer off, or he would let everyone know the real me. There he was—trying to feed off the fact he thought I was scared of all that I had done, the past I was. He had not realized that girl was long dead. I knew I was forgiven, and there was now no condemnation for me. I was no longer the things I had done, a prisoner of my past held down by chains. I knew this, and I believed it!

We were without cable, and that was fine. I took that time to go deeper with God. I started reading daily devotionals, morning and night. I joined a group at church and started a forty-day study. I started renewing my mind daily with God's Word, and my faith began to grow even more. I was isolated in my home with no cable, no Internet; I did not have a smartphone, and I did not go out. I was able to shut out the noise of the world and focus on my faith and grow to know God's love for me. I needed God more than ever to get me through the times I had ahead. When the kids were with their dad, I was home alone with the dog and the cat. I was alone but never lonely. This was a great time for me to get saturated in God's love. My faith was growing, and everything was starting to make sense. I had not seen my counselor in a while because of what Jack was saying about him before I moved out.

I TRUST YOU, LORD

We had the PDL hearing to settle visitation and child support. Jack showed up with Gwen. I sat in the lobby outside the courtroom by myself, but I was not alone. I had this little booklet of verses my mother had given me. I read Psalm 23 over and over while I waited that lobby:

> The Lord is my shepherd, I shall not be in want. He makes me lie down in green pastures; he leads me beside quiet waters; He restores my soul. He quides me in right paths for his name's sake. Even though I walk through the valley of the shadow of death, I fear no evil for you are with me, your rod and your staff they comfort me. You prepare a table before me in the presence of my enemies you anoint my head with oil; my cup overflows. Surely goodness and mercy shall follow me all the days of my life, and I shall dwell in the house of the Lord forever.
>
> Psalm 23:2–6 (NIV)

I kept repeating it to myself until I was calmed down. I was saying it and believing it; it was settling into my heart. I could hear Gwen and Jack talking and laughing across the way, but I was fine—God was with me. My lawyer came out of chambers and said that the judge wants us on the stand. He said that is usually never the case, but he wanted to hear from both of us. I was calm. *His rod and his staff comfort me.* The seal right above the judge's head on the wall read In God We Trust. I read it and said "amen" under my breath. Before we proceeded, the judge asked for Gwen to leave the courtroom since this matter did not pertain to her. Jack's lawyer said, "Your Honor, I'd like for her to also take the stand." The judge said, "There is no need for me to hear from her counselor." Yes, *your rod and staff comfort me*.

I took the stand, and I was attacked by Jack's lawyer with questions asking me about my drinking and about the medications I was on. I answered, and I would tend to elaborate on each answer. He went on to talk ask about Olivia's dental surgery. He was implying neglect on my part. I stayed calm and explained what happened. This man was really trying to paint an ugly portrait of some person I no longer knew. I could feel the attacking nature of the questions, and I answered them—but not in a defensive way as I would normally. I was drawing on the Holy Spirit who dwelled inside me. He was giving me peace and the words to say. I remember once I answered a question, and I heard what sounded like the court reporter sitting next to me on the stand, kind of whispering "amen" under her breath. I knew somehow God had my back, and it did not matter what that lawyer made me look like.

Jack got on the stand, very confident and cocky. He went on and on about all the things Gwen did for the kids that I never did, about how she was a great cook and on and on. My lawyer asked him why she needed to live there. Jack answered along the lines of since his hours are all over the place, he needed her handy to make him a sandwich if needed. So my lawyer made a point of saying, "So she is there strictly to fulfill your needs and not the children's?" My lawyer asked why this housekeeper did not just have regular work hours on certain days and then just go home after that. My lawyer was good, and I just marveled at how he was able to make the Goliath in my life just crumble. Jack threw out quite a few accusations about me; I had no idea of what he was even talking about. When the criticism does not make any sense, it is not about you, it is a spiritual battle, so just let God fight for you. One could just feel the arrogance he had about the whole thing. Even the way he sat in the chair on the stand, all leaned back as if he was in complete control. He failed to read the seal on the wall above the judge. God has the ultimate control.

I was completely calm during the entire thing. The Holy Spirit had given me peace that surpassed my understanding. We ran out of time, so the judge said he would render a decision by the end of the week. My lawyer told me that I talked too much on the stand, but it was a good thing.

The rest of that day, I would go over everything that was said in court in my head over and over, trying to remember how it all went. Some of the things Jack said about me hurt, but I knew that I was no longer that girl he was describing. He said I never cooked, that my house was dirty, and on and on. I tried to fill my mind with truth, and delete the bad memory. I was operating off a new hardware system, and that old operating system was outdated. I had to repeat these things in my head over and over. The scriptures I was learning in my group at church would come up in my mind and comfort me. I needed to shut out the doubt, worry, and anxiety. I was told in class that God speaks to us using his Word, so it was very important to know his Word, by reading the Bible. They were right! I was able to cling to these words of truth to quiet and calm my soul:

> Trust in the Lord with all your heart and lean not on your own understanding; in all ways acknowledge him, and he will make your paths straight.
>
> Proverbs 3:5–6 (NIV)

> Give all your worries and cares to God, for he cares about you.
>
> 1 Peter5:7 (NIV)

The time came later that week, and I got something from the court in the mail. My hand was shaking. I opened it, I read it, and we got everything we wanted. The visitation schedule was changed, and the amount of child support we asked for was accepted. I dropped to my knees and said, "Thank you, Jesus!" God will do as he sees fit. Amen.

I got a text from Jack asking about the schedule for the weekend. I told him to read his paperwork. He said there was no paperwork. I assured him there was. He said he called his lawyer, and he had nothing. He had checked online, and there was nothing posted. I told him I was holding the paperwork in my hand. He told me that was impossible, that I was lying. I remember at that point double-checking to make sure it was the right paperwork with the right names and that is was not some sort of mistake. That was the kind of control he had over me that I had to fully break away from. I had the papers in my hand, yet I still doubted because he said I was a liar. I needed to still grow and learn that it only mattered what God said I was, and not what anyone else said or thought of me. I had been given the righteousness of Jesus, and my sins were paid for. The wreckage of my past no longer held me down—I was set free.

GOD REALLY IS LOVE

Things were going much better. Gina was now preparing to go on leave of absence, so it was now time for her to train me for her job she did in the back. While she was on leave, I would not be at the front desk. We would hire a temporary employee to work the desk where I was working. Things between her and I were going great. Mindy and I were not really getting along very well at all. My new approach was to ignore her completely. I would not let her have power over my emotions, so I would simply not have any. Gina assured me that was not going to work, and I needed a better resolve before she left to go on her leave. I would use Gina as a buffer, but when she left, I would not have her anymore. I now worked at a desk in very close proximity to Mindy. I would not talk to her or even look at her. I would send an e-mail if I needed to have contact with her. She would always reply back. Then, more and more, I would think about my faith and listen to great teachers talk about extending grace to others and not to take offense from others. I was learning also that gossip was very sinful behavior. When we engage in doing those things, we block our own blessings, and that also leaves a stronghold for the devil to get in and cause even bigger problems. God was working with me here. I needed to learn the lesson and do things His way and not my way.

I prayed for God to show me how to handle the situation with Mindy at work. I decided I would extend an olive branch to Mindy, to preserve the bond of peace. I had heard her talk about wanting to get in shape, so I offered to train her and another girl to see how they would like it, for no charge. She accepted, and I was so excited to get the opportunity to work with her on my level of expertise, so to speak. Mindy was extremely proficient in her job, and was the go-to person for people in all different departments. She was a master problem solver. My defensive behavior- which came about as a resultof her always correcting me- was the root of our differences. I thought perhaps if we got on my playing field, things could really be different between us. The day came for us to do the workout. That morning, she came in and let me know she was not in the mood, and it was not going to work. I was crushed. I felt completely rejected by this woman. I so desperately wanted to change things between us, and I felt like that was the ultimate rejection. I did not communicate this to her, yet I did not let it consume me. I cast the worry and stress that began to take hold of me at the foot of the cross. I did what God put on my heart to do; he would take care of the rest.

I was really starting to set my heart to yield to God. I was amazed at how he was working with me. For the first time in my life, it was like the things that were happening around me were teaching me things about myself. These were painful realities that I would have to work on to become more Christ-like. The more and more I focused on what that meant, the more I became like him in my thinking. I was learning to extend grace and to look at people's hearts more. People act the way they do a lot of times because of their own underlying issues, that have nothing to do with me. God was showing me that the way people reacted to me was not because of some sort of default within me. I was learning not to take things personally. He was growing me up to see that, and helping me to erase all the negative thoughts I had about myself. Little by little, he was giving me my power back. For so long, I was giving it away to people to control how I behaved and reacted to situations in my life.

Gina had to leave early one day, so I had to cover the front desk that afternoon. In walks the Christian counselor I had stopped seeing. He did not realize I worked there. His office was right up the street, and he said he was not sure if this was the building where he could sign up for a gym membership. I told him no he would have to do that at the center. We both knew it was a Holy Spirit thing that he would just so happen to come in at a time I would normally not even be up front. I now started to realize things that happened around me—and to me, they were no longer coincidences. I paid attention more to things. I looked for a lesson in everything. I was no longer just floating haphazardly through life. I told him I would call him for an appointment.

Things were the same with Jack. We would go back and forth with the bickering. I would work so hard to not respond to him. He paid me fifty dollars more than he had to in child support monthly to show good faith, but whenever things were not going the way he wanted, he would pay the lower amount the court ordered. He was using this as a form of control. He would send text messages, and I would just ignore him. I was taking my power back. I would no longer allow him to control my mood—it was that simple. I was learning self-control in the matter. I would pray about it, and God would give me the strength to deal with it. Prayer was how I got through all of this. I would just talk to God. Tell him exactly how I felt about everything. I would yell sometimes and cry other times. I knew he was listening. I could actually feel his warmth comfort me. Remember, I was the girl who by now would have been cozying up to another man to fulfill the need for love deep within me. Getting to know God and letting him heal my wounds and fill the void was all I needed. Dating was not even on my mind. I was under a full remodel job. God was gutting out my insides and making me new from the inside out, and showing me his love for me the entire time.

By now, my relationship with my brother was really good. He was happy to see me living on my own with a good job. He was going to church also, so we would talk about the great things God was doing in our lives. Whenever I did get lonely, I would go to his apartment and watch a movie and hang out with him. I did not have a washer and dryer, so I would do laundry at his apartment complex. I tried not to talk about Jack all the time, but that seemed to be what I would do. I would vent and tell my brother the latest thing he did. I did not realize this, but just by talking about it, I was giving the situation power over me. My brother would constantly just change the subject. He could see my struggle.

He had so many books in his apartment that they took up an entire wall. He did not have TV at his house either, only a DVD player with a projector. He would read a lot and drown out the noise of the world. Out of all the books he had, he went right over and gave me a brand new book he had on forgiveness. It was a small book. He told me to read it and then tell him what I thought about it.

It was Valentine's Day, and Jack came over to get the kids that evening. They were already in the car when he came back to the door. He was acting really weird. He was telling me how he knew I still loved him and that if I just gave him a kiss, I would really realize it. I had no idea what he was talking about. He was coaxing me to kiss him and somehow I was hugging him when I grabbed his jacket pocket, and there was a tape recorder. Ha! He was stunned I found it. I asked him, "What was that?" I asked him what he was trying to pull? He had no words. He only shook his head and left. That same night, I started reading the book *The Gift of Forgiveness* by Paul J. Meyer on February 14th of 2012. It was my very first Valentine's Day without a Valentine. I opened the book with a glass of wine. This book was exactly what I needed! It talked about setting yourself free from what others have done to you over the years. This was huge for me. We cannot fully understand how we are forgiven if we do not extend forgiveness to others. It causes us to hold on to bitterness, and also it was a stronghold for the devil to get in and make messes of our lives. I had a long list of people to forgive. The book talked about how a lot of times the people we need to forgive have no idea they had even hurt you. That would be the case for my mother. They are going on about their life oblivious while we sit there and suffer. The book had me recall every offender who hurt me and every hurt I had endured. I wrote it down. It did not mean I condoned what was done to me. I was simply freeing myself from allowing it to hurt me any longer. I wrote out my lists and then I burned the papers I wrote it on. This signified that I have forgiven the offense, and it is buried and over with—you do not dig it back up. I had to do this part over and over every time it would come up. I learned to tear people a new clean sheet every day. This was a major breakthrough in my life, and on Valentine's Day, it was a perfect gift of love from my baby brother. I was carrying so much anger, resentment, and bitterness, and a lot of it was aimed toward me. After I was able to do this for myself, things really began to change.

The next couple of weekends went by, and I got the chance to spend some time with my brother. I let him know that the book really helped me, and the timing was perfect. I was actually able to spend time with my brother without talking about the latest incident with Jack. We went shopping at the thrift store that day, my little cousin and his friend were with us. I saw a couch with a double recliner for eighty dollars. This couch was in great condition. We needed a new couch since the one that was given to us was wearing out. I did not go to that store that day intending to buy a couch. I kept looking at it and thinking, *I am just going to get it*. I told my brother, and he checked it out. He thought it was a really good deal also. Both recliners worked on it, and it was clean and everything. The only thing he was thinking about was how we would get it home. That thought did not even cross my mind. My bother had a mid-sized SUV, and we had two kids with us. He told me not to worry about it and to have faith. I paid for the couch, and then four guys who worked in the back brought it out to the car. They all said, "There is no way this couch will fit in there." Remember, this is what these guys did all day—fit things into people's cars. My brother was busy moving things around and laying the seats down to make room for the couch, as if he did not even hear their negativity. I was in agreement with them, shaking my head too. My brother had faith that it would fit. He told me, "Faith is the evidence of things hoped for and yet to be seen. We live by faith and not by sight." He was right. I snapped out of my disbelief and started helping him get things situated. We had God's favor, and we had to believe that, even at this very moment. He told the guys how to lift it in and put the couch on its side. They did what he said—and it fit! We all stood there in disbelief. We were even able to fit the kids in with the couch for the short ride home. That was the perfect testimony of faith.

I got a call from Jack telling me that Gwen was not going to be working for him anymore, and that she would be moving out that weekend. I had been praying about this situation, and even though I could not see anything happening, it was apparent that God was working on it. Apparently, Gwen had lied to Jack about something, so he had to let her go. That was all the detail he gave me. I really did not care; I was just glad she was going to be gone. He also assured me that he would not be hiring anyone else to take her place. He told me I was right—that it was just wrong to have someone move in like that. I was relieved. From then on, we started talking more civil to each other.

I found myself witnessing to him about the changes God had made in me. He would actually listen to me. During this time, I was wondering, *What is God showing me?* Was I the one he was working on to bring about change in my husband? There had been many delays in our divorce. My lawyer left the country for a month, and then when he returned, he got caught up in a manslaughter trial. Was God trying to delay things to give us time to heal, to work this out? I was not sure, but I knew that if it was his will, it would be done. I was seeing my counselor again, and he felt the same way about the situation. It was his prayer that things would work out, and that the Lord would restore the marriage.

Jack went out and got a new Bible he was telling me about it. He marveled at how different I was. He could tell I was not the same. He started going to church. I would invite him over for Sunday dinners. He would drop the kids at 6 p.m. every other Sunday, and we would all have dinner together. It was nothing more than that. I was very honest with him and told him that I had no sexual feelings for him. I was interested in getting to know him in a way I never had before. This offended him, only because I used to be a total physical person no matter what. We would argue in the past but still had no problem having sex while being mad at each other. Maybe he really did not see the change in me. I was very serious. I was all about looking at his heart. I was choosing to let God help me become a better person, and I was hopeful he wanted the same thing for himself. God worked within me and took away the sinful sexual force that used to drive all of my actions. Talk about a major remodel job! After that comment I made, and he realized I was serious, we stopped with the dinners with the kids. I guess he still felt like he had to punish me every time something did not go his way. He was still using the same old operating system.

God gently showed me through this that Jack never loved me the way God intended for me to be loved. I also never loved him. I began to now mourn the loss of the relationship I had with Jack. We spent so much of our time and effort with it, and all the while it was not real love. It was something we felt for each other that we attached our meaning of love to. I now know that love is so much more than a feeling. God is love. I did not know the love of God, and so there was no way I could ever fulfill the covenant of love with my husband the way it was meant to be. I began to think about all the things love is and how I had not experienced most of these with Jack.

> Love is patient, Love is kind, Love does not envy, Love does not boast, Love is not proud, Love is not rude, Love always trusts, Love always hopes and Love never fails.
>
> 1 Corinthians 13:4–8 (NIV)

By this time, I was able to handle whatever Jack threw my way. I was studying the Word, and I was in a women's support group at church. I had all kinds of support around me. I was listening to Christian radio; I had completely stopped listening to secular radio. I listened to spiritual leader's podcasts while I worked out. My faith was growing. I was being renewed. I did make the mistake of sharing with Jack what I had learned about love and what we shared in comparison. That did not make for good conversation in the least. I was open to learn and discuss the topic, but he was all about accusing and telling me I had no idea what he felt for me (case in point).

I got baptized in April 2012. Over the Easter weekend, my brother, my mother, Chloe, and Olivia were there. We are commanded to believe and then be baptized. This symbolizes us dying to our old way of life or a life of our own flesh, and being raised up as a new creation in Christ. Getting baptized for me was now the start of me walking out my faith wherever I went. We celebrated by going to the Christian bookstore. I got a cross bracelet, and Mom got me a bookmark. We then had dinner all together. It was really nice. I felt so excited for what was yet to come in my new life as a believer.

The challenge would be when I was at work. I knew every day I would have to deny my flesh and let the Holy Spirit lead me. There were certain things I used to do that I could no longer tolerate. I no longer used foul language, and when I heard others use it, it would really bother me. I was in the habit of talking about my divorce—and bad mouthing Jack and the entire situation. I began to change my language and thoughts. There were always sarcastic remarks to be made at work; I would try to refrain from chiming in. There was plenty of complaining and grumbling around me for the most part of any day. I would work toward not being dragged into negative conversations and gossip. I tried to look for the positive in everything. I would be the one to want to give the benefit of the doubt in situations that bothered others. I felt like good would always outweigh the bad. I felt like the people who did others wrong at work would eventually get what they deserved, and it was not my place to point out and complain about the wrongdoings of others. God will do as he sees fit. He has the final say in all things. It was as if God put me right in the mecca for all those types of things in this new job. He put me where people were just being people, carrying out their lives, speaking how they speak. My eyes and ears were opened to the negativity that just seemed to be so routine for others. I was more mindful of it, and it began to disturb me. God was indeed making me new. I used to chime right in with stuff. I now had an awareness of it and would remain silent and just try to focus on the positive things around me.

I was invited to go down to the river with my coworker Dee and another coworker, who was a Christian named Sarah. Dee had a cabin down there. It was a weekend I did not have kids and I would be able to bring the dog. She had asked me several times if I would go, and there really was no reason I couldn't. I was able to make my own decision about it without getting permission, and that felt great. I was excited to get away for a bit of a girls' weekend. The weekends without the kids were always especially hard for me. I did not go out at all, and every now and then, I'd get insecure about why I was alone, sitting on the couch. Then I would realize I was never alone.

We had only planned to stay one night and float the river one day. Sarah did not drink, and Dee really did not either. Sarah had brought along her teenage daughter and her friend. I felt good about having a wholesome time away. I loved being out in the sun; I have always loved the way it felt on my skin. We got there and got settled in. We made a fire and relaxed. The dog loved it. She took off running; there was plenty of open area for her to do that. She consumed the country air. Dee was all about preparing the wood and the canoes, and Sarah was busy making dinner for us. We had chicken kabobs, and they were delicious. It was peaceful.

The next day, we got out on the river. The water was kind of low, so there were times we had to drag the canoes over the shallow parts. Along the way, Sarah was looking for pieces of petrified wood to go in her garden. She had an artistic eye and knew exactly what she was looking for. About two miles down the river, she saw a perfect piece. We pulled up to where it was. This was a pretty good-sized piece of wood. She kept eyeing it, knowing it was exactly what she was looking for. But she was not sure if it would fit in the canoe and how to get it back. We had had about two more miles to go. Then I told her the story of my brother and the couch. I told her if there is a will, there is a way. "Faith is the evidence of things hoped for and not yet seen, we live by faith and not by sight." With that she said, "You're right." I got out and helped her lift this heavy, awkward piece of wood, and we got it in her canoe. She would have to now sit in the front part of the canoe with her legs straddling the sides. Sarah is a marathon runner and was in very good shape. She had no problem rowing the canoe with the extra weight of that piece of wood. She got it all the way back, and we loaded it in the truck. We could not believe it. She said she would have just left it there without the little reminder I gave her. God is good, and having faith in him in all things is so awesome.

TRAIN ME UP TO DO YOUR WILL

It came time for Gina to go on leave, and so the temp person who worked the desk now was a girl I knew from when I worked at the center. She was such a blessing. She was a Christian, so we shared our faith together. I'd talk to her about different problems I was having in the divorce, and she would always have words of encouragement. She would share different Bible passages, and we'd talk about sermons we heard every week. It felt good to have someone at work whom I could talk about my faith with. Just by talking to this woman, it seemed I started to attract other Christians around me in the workplace, whom I did not realize were believers. That was exciting to me. Since I had this connection with the new temporary member of the team, I think that this irritated the relationship I had with Mindy. I would tread lightly with her extending grace often. I even tried to help her out with some of the extra work she had. The city had experienced a weather disaster that called for an influx of permit applications, so at this time the customer service team was under quite a bit of extra paperwork. I would take some overtime hours just to try and keep ahead of the workload. Mindy asked me to do some of her work for her to help her. I was so honored that she would ask me to help her with something.

I was seeing the Christian counselor regularly again. He was impressed with my progress. I had weaned myself with his guidance off all my medications. I was no longer on any medication. I saw him every two weeks, so he was able to make sure he did not see any behaviors of concern. This was a huge relief for me. I knew the battle for my mind was over.

"Your faith has made you well, go in peace and be healed of your affliction." (Mark 5:34, NIV)

Since I was under so much stress before, I had really bad acne that no medication would clear up. My dermatologist was ready to put me on an extreme med since nothing we tried was working. I also had bad back pain. Since I put my faith in God and cast all the burdens of anxiety and stress onto him, I literally was able to relieve my body from the effects of stress. My back issues were no more, and the acne cleared up also. I no longer had anxiety or depression or insomnia.

"A peaceful heart leads to a healthy body." (Proverbs 14:30, NIV)

I started to be more aware of the people around complaining about being sick all the time and having to take all kinds of medications. I now could see the link. It was their heart. If you have true whole peace in your heart, you really should not have so many problems with your health. Issues like insomnia, depression, gastrointestinal, stress-related issues like high blood pressure and the like. When you are stressed, the body puts off an excess of hormones that can be damaging to other parts of the body, and can cause all kinds of other problems. Peace in the heart dissipates the stress that causes havoc on our bodies. If there is also a real appreciation for the life you are given by God, you will do all you can to take care of your body. You will respect yourself enough to lead a healthy lifestyle. This can only start within. I honestly believe that, and this was my own personal experience. Once I was rooted in Christ and accepted his peace, literally all my aliments left my body. I knew who I was in him and that he died to set me free from the chains of anxiety, depression, doubt, fear, and the like. He carries my burdens so I do not have to. I had to constantly remind myself of this every day.

I came into work, and I was at my desk. I could see Mindy talking to our boss. She was waving her arms around, and it was very clear she was upset. I could hear her saying, "That is why it is always easier for me to just do things myself. People around here don't understand how to do things correctly." I was sure now she was talking about me. Did she not see I was right there, not even five feet from her? She was going on and on about something I messed up. I felt humiliated—surely there was a more tactful way to handle this, whatever it was I did. Later my boss came to me and explained that I made some errors in the payments I posted for the paperwork, which I stayed late to do the night before for Mindy. It was not fully explained to me that the payment would not automatically post to the correct payee, which I had to make sure it was, and if it was not, I'd have to input the information. I was given literally hundreds of these to do, and I was so proud I was able to get them completed. This was a major detail. I do not think the importance of it was explained to me. I am not a clerical whiz; doing this job was a major stretch for me. My boss told me not to worry about it, that things could be corrected. I was crushed. I was happy to help Mindy with something, and then I ended up messing the whole thing up.

That incident created an even bigger wedge between us. She was now not talking or even looking at me. When I worked back at my desk, I would have my earphones on. I would spend the day listening to podcasts by Joyce Meyer, James McDonald, T. D. Jakes, and Joel Osteen. I would fill my head with God's word. I knew that faith only comes by hearing God's Word. It was remarkable to me that I would go to church and hear a message and then listen to other teachers of the word, and they were all saying the same thing. There was no confusion because they were all using the same book. This was awesome learning for me because they each had a way of saying the same thing, and it would all resonate in my heart and provoke change in me every day.

I would also spend some time talking with the temp girl. Now she was in the middle of Mindy and I, just like Gina was. Mindy would now ask the temp to help her with her extra workload, and not me. That really hurt, but God was reminding me it was not about me. I made a mistake, but that did not mean I was worthless like I was being treated. The temp girl being there was another extension of the body of Christ reaching out to me. The timing of her being placed in the situation was all part of his plan. I would pray every day about the situation with Mindy. It was an awkwardly horrible feeling to go to work with such tension in the air day after day. I was the one whom everyone liked before; this was definitely God showing me that I only needed to worry about pleasing him and not people.

I learned from listening to Joyce that sowing discord with others was an abomination to God. We were supposed to get along with other people on purpose. It was wrong to get offended by our own insecurities. I was trying so hard to walk that out in my own life. I was giving everyone grace around me by tearing them a clean page every day. This was especially difficult with Jack.

There were other people in the office who clearly started to show their dislike for me as well. I had a meeting with my boss about a complaint that he received from someone who was not even in our department. I was told in that meeting by my boss, "You are doing something very right if the theses certain people are complaining." I was told very simply to keep doing what I was doing. That was huge for me. I was essentially being told that not everyone will like me, and everyone will always have something negative to say, but that only shows that the good I was doing was only irritating the people who did not matter anyway. God was showing me more things about me every day. The different situations I encountered were proof of that. Being in the light will cause the ones in darkness to be uncomfortable.

I remember being in a meeting and having the head of the department yell at me regarding a matter where I took my customer service skills further than he would have liked. I knew I was not wrong in how I responded in the matter. My boss and my boss's boss had already commended me on the action I took. I knew at the time of the meeting my being yelled at had nothing to do with me. It was entirely about the other person. That person needed to look strong in front of everyone by making me look weak and inferior. After the meeting, when no one was around, I did get an apology, which further proved the intent. God was so good at what *he* was showing me. I was in training at this job for something great. The old Cassie Booth would have crumbled under that kind of attack. I was seeing things completely different; I was maturing, and it felt great.

I was starting to get irritated with being known as a personal trainer. The time I would spend with the girls on my lunch break was not as fulfilling as it once was. I started really wanting my lunch break time as an actual break from that place. I was also having issues with feeling that the girls not really taking my time seriously. They were not reaching their goals, and it seemed that the workout group was more of a social hour for them, and I was taking that personally. They were not paying me very much, so there really was no value attached to it for them either. I started cancelling sessions and before long, I was not training the group anymore. I was not training anyone. I was no longer a trainer in my mind. That was always my identity before, but I was being shown that I was so much more than that label I was carrying. God was really showing me something now. He just took personal training away from my heart just like that. I still worked out and ate healthy; I just was not a trainer.

I was getting my running in, but I was not as adamant about it as I was before in my life when I was "running from something." I wanted to complete a marathon later in the year, but I started to think about why that was so important to me. God was showing me that he loved me the same, whether I ran that race or not. My self-worth was not in the number of miles I ran. My brother would ask me each week how many miles I ran. I found it to be more of an annoyance than encouragement or motivation. I was no longer defined by being a personal trainer or by the distance I would run each week. These were two things I took quite a bite of *pride* in the past, but it just did not seem to fit me anymore. God was emptying me of myself and filling me up with him.

Around this time, I also cut all my hair very, very short. I got it cut shorter than I ever had in my life. It was less than an inch short all over. I did this to really humble myself. For years, it was so important to me how I looked, and having nice hair and a nice body were all very superficial things that really meant nothing when my heart was just bad. God was revamping me completely. I was getting the overhauling I so long needed and desired. Even with very short hair, I was able to see – thanks to God- that I was more beautiful than ever. My inner beauty began to shine through.

Meanwhile, the divorce was still not final. Jack still had kept his word and did not hire another housekeeper. At this point, he wanted things in the divorce final. He was ready to move on; he was tired of being lonely, he had told me. I was fine with it. I knew God was doing amazing things in my life, and he was all I needed. The kids were doing well. They loved church, and they could tell I was much happier than I had been in a long time.

There was some time lapse with the divorce between his lawyer and mine. Jack asked me to have my lawyer draft something up and he would sign. I had an appointment scheduled, and I left work to get to the law office and hit a huge traffic jam. The highway was at a standstill. I called the law office, and since it was a late appointment anyway, the receptionist advised me to reschedule, but there would not be anything for a couple of weeks. I saw this as a sign from God. Jack accused me of stalling; everything always had to be my fault in his eyes. Perhaps time is what was needed to work on Jack's heart in the matter. I had peace, so whatever the plan was, I was going to be fine with it.

Meanwhile, work was still very busy. Mindy and I were somewhat better. I had humbled myself and apologized to her. I explained I never intended to do anything but to help her. I was truly sorry that my mistake caused such an issue for her. She seemed to accept my apology, so we were off to a clean slate again.

We seemed to be off on the right path. However, that same week out of the blue, another coworker brought it to my attention something that was overheard about me. It really did not bother me since it seemed like someone always had something to say about me, no matter what I did. This time, I did get physically sick soon after I was given the information. All I wanted to do was get out of that place and go home to my little house on Harmony Lane. I sent an e-mail to my boss that I needed to leave. I got the okay, so I left for the day. It was like one thing after another at work. I was walking closely with God, and it just seemed like wave after wave of resistance would come against me, either from coworkers or Jack. I felt helpless and overwhelmed. I felt like I was being persecuted, and my heart had nothing but the purest of intentions in all circumstances. I went to the temp, and she prayed with me at the desk. She assured me that this was indeed Satan trying to get in between her and I. She said if he divides us, he can conquer. Was she right? I believed her, but I also had doubts about what she was saying.

I got home and went for a run with the dog and my iPod, and filled my head with God's word. I was able to get centered on God. I remembered he is made strong in my weakness. I began to realize that the sick feeling I had was God's way of shining a light on the realization that what others say about me does not matter. He knows my heart, and I live for him, and that is enough. My flesh was weak, but I had to remain focused on his love for me, and he would make my paths straight. I knew that I was being put in the fire to be molded into someone God could use to do great things. I knew these things were not just randomly happening to me without a reason.

I had support all around me. I was able to talk to a good friend on the phone who was also a Christian. She said many things that affirmed God's love for me. I was thankful she took the time out to talk to me. I had decided to take another day off work. I was not ready to go back just yet. I spent the next day fasting and in prayer. God knew my heart, and I needed his strength to get me through all of the devil's schemes to try and take me out. I was able to get in and see my counselor that day also. He gave me more assurance that God's love was all around me. He said God would always give me protection and guidance. I would be able to go back to work armed with his righteousness, and I would be vindicated.

I returned to work. I was prayed up and ready for whatever came at me next. I knew God had my back and whatever battle I faced was already won. The most remarkable answer to my prayer had happened next. I was told that Mindy would be moved from the customer service department. I was told things were going back to the way they were years ago. Most of what Mindy handled was signed off in the clerk's office anyway, so she would be moving to the clerk's office effective in two weeks. Wow! Just like that, a problem was solved. This move would also be good for Mindy as well. Now she could focus on the main thing she was very good at, and not have to be bothered with worrying about a team. This immediately resolved all of our conflict. I congratulated her on her promotion. She was very nervous but excited all at once. It was like God just gave us both another clean slate with each other. We were getting along great now.

Gina returned back from her leave. She was almost sickened to see how well Mindy and I were getting along. Our relationship had done a complete turn around, to say the least. I could not believe it at times either. I did not have to fake it. I was genuinely able to get along with her with a freshness I could not explain; it was in fact the Holy Spirit living with in me.

Things with the divorce were still creeping along. By this time, Jack had moved one of his brothers into his house with him. He had fallen on some hard times, so Jack was there to help him out. Jack was the big brother to nine siblings. He was always very good at coming to the aid if any of them ever needed any help. He was a protector; it was in his nature. The girls were thrilled to have time with their cousins whenever they spent time with their dad. It was fun for them.

The sessions with my counselor were getting deeper. We were digging more into my past and bringing things into light that were very painful to talk about. I was discovering why I was promiscuous as a teen. I identified how my mother raised me, and the identity crisis I lived with in not knowing who I was. It was all flooding in. God was showing me that the life I lived was not my fault. My identity was stolen. I never had my identity in Christ; my identity was rooted in false things. I started to think about how my grandpa impacted my life and how his love for me was the closest thing to what I have with God. It was amazing how all these revelations were becoming so clear to me now. It was all fitting together in my mind so clearly.

I took time away from talking to my mother. I told her I was going through some things regarding my past, and I just needed some time. I assured her that I loved her and that things would be fine. God was working with me on a few things, and everything would be fine in time. I am not really sure how she felt about that, but I knew I did really need the time.

Mindy had moved to a different part of the building. They did not hire the temp on as full time, and now Gina was back. The customer service team was now just her and I. We had decided we would both stay up at the front desk and run it together. We got along well, and that made things easier if we were both together. Gina was one who always had something witty to say and used foul language on occasion. It did not bother me before because I also talked the same way. Now that I was growing in my faith, it was a completely different story. The constant sarcasm was becoming offensive to me. I think she could tell a difference in my behavior. Whenever other coworkers would come to the desk to gossip or complain, I would just remain silent and mind my own business instead of chiming in. Most times, people would automatically assume something was wrong with me because I opted out of the conversation. That would make me laugh to myself—to think that they would think something was wrong with me, doing what is righteous. Before long, I started to feel somewhat oppressed working at the desk. I had a sense of heaviness all around me. It truly bothered me that Gina would literally laugh about everything. Even if it was a serious problem, she would find a way to make light of it—with laughter. I started to realize that maybe her laughter was a way to hide her pain. I found myself sharing different things I would learn in different Bible teachings I listened to with her. I would share scripture that I had read or different podcasts that I had heard to try and help her. I planted the seed, and I prayed God would take care of the rest.

Gina was someone I told everything to. She was there from the start of the divorce procedure. She was someone I genuinely cared about. God was showing me that I needed to confide in people who were focused on eternity, like I was. Friends on earth are fine, but friends that you will have throughout eternity are even better. I knew Gina was not saved. She believed there is a God but questioned creation. She was not saved. She had never even read the Bible. We talked about that. I know that the only way to get to heaven is through accepting the blood of Jesus Christ as the atonement for our sin, that it was a free gift for whosoever believed. I was not sure she fully understood that. When certain things would happen in my life, she would always just think they were coincidences. I would tell her that there are no coincidences with God; that everything works together for good in the life of a believer. I invited her to church and to different Bible studies, but she never was able to make it. She thought all the importance was surrounded by the Virgin Mary. I tried to explain to her that Mary was just an ordinary woman whom God used to do something great. She was a vessel he used just as all of us are called to be. I do not think she was able to make that connection. I explained that it is not about religion but all about relationship with God. Jesus died so we could have communion with the Father. Having a relationship with Christ is not just a way you act; it is an ongoing experience in growth. The more you behold him, the more you become like him. Old ways pass away, and things become new. I was no longer comfortable speaking and acting a way that was not worthy of the Gospel. This was a growth process, and as I became stronger in the Lord, the temptations of sin would fall away.

There was a weekend that Gina invited me to go to a wedding in her small hometown. She was excited to get away, to see her family and have a weekend to party with old friends. When she first asked me, I said, "Oh yeah. Sure." Then the Holy Spirit started stirring within me. I knew it was not something for me. It was not somewhere I needed to be going. First of all, the small town she is from is a very tight-knit community where there were not many black people. I did not want to be put in a situation where I did not know anyone and then forced to work at gaining acceptance, like I was so used to doing in my past. Then I also knew I did not need to be in an environment of drunkenness and carousing that was in no way appealing to me. There was also a women's conference at my church that same weekend. The choice of where I'd rather be and where I should be was made very plainly to me. I sent Gina an e-mail explaining all of this. I was much more comfortable expressing my thoughts in words on a page then I could face to face. She told me she completely understood, and it was fine. She was always so easygoing about everything.

Later that same week, I went to lunch with a coworker I would normally go to lunch with on occasion, either with just him or a group of us. He was an older married man who worked in the same department. He was always very helpful at the desk whenever we would need him to come out and talk to a customer. He was also someone who had a vast amount of knowledge about most everything. He prided himself in knowing things. This particular time we went to lunch was very different. We went to a place that was actually a bar. There were all men there, mostly blue-collared workers. There was smoke in the air, and there were waitresses wearing skimpy shorts and low-cut blouses. All the men around me were stealing glances at them whenever they could. I was the only female patron in the entire place. I was utterly disgusted and extremely uncomfortable. The Holy Spirit was definitely stirring within me; I knew that I had matured in my faith. I knew that I did not belong in a place like that. I knew that if the person who I was with really knew me, and knew my relationship with God, he would have not even suggested we eat there. In my past, I would have never even thought twice about being in an atmosphere like that. God was giving me revelation that the girl of my past indeed was dead and I was a new creature in him.

Jack's brother moved in with his two kids. He was having some serious issues in his marriage. He would not be in a position to help Jack much with anything until he was situated with a car and job. Our kids were excited to have their cousins to play with whenever they went to visit their dad. Having his brother there was also helpful to Jack when he did have the girls since his work schedule was still at times unpredictable.

I was working with the law office on drafting a settlement agreement. I was e-mailed the draft of what it would be, and I cringed at the numbers that were on it. We were asking for maintenance, child support, and a settlement fee, and I knew that Jack would not agree to it. My lawyer assured me we needed to start high to leave room for negotiating. I had to also remember Jack made almost four times more than I did. He owned two homes, and I would have both our kids—one who had special needs—most of the time. I still did not feel right about the amount, so I lowered it in my mind. Somehow I did not feel deserving of it, yet I was put through so much. But then again, I did not have a vindictive heart. God would take care of the offenses of others. I would take time to think it over and get back with my lawyer. Of course, then I took the time to discuss this with some people from work. They were all giving the advice more or less to get all I could, and take my feelings out of it. This was all pretty much "unchurched" advice. Listen to no man who fails to listen to God.

I had planned to get the girls in the kids Bible program at our church. The parent information meeting was scheduled for that night. It was planned that the parents would meet for dinner and then there would be a meeting to follow. I explained to Jack that the girls would need to stay later at his house that evening until the meeting concluded at about 8 p.m. I had even given him the flyer with all the information on it. I was at the meeting really liking what I was hearing. They had introduced all the leaders who would be helping the kids. They did a special prayer after that. During the prayer, my cell phone was going crazy in my purse. It was on vibrate, but I could tell it was going off. After the prayer, I checked my phone, and I had several messages from Jack, asking where I was. It was only about 7:30, and we had not gone on the tour yet. I stepped out into the hallway and called him back. He was very angry with me. He was saying he had to leave for work and did not understand why it was taking so long. His brother was there at the house with the kids, and I told him I would be there before eight to get them, so I was not sure what the problem was. He was cursing me out and eventually hung up on me. I left the church right after that and picked the girls up. I spoke with Jack's brother when I got there since Jack had already left for work. I told his brother I was sorry for any inconvenience, and that Jack knew I would be done before eight. His brother assured me there was no problem and everything was fine.

The kids and I got home and settled in for the night. It was revealed to me that it did not matter what I did; Jack would always be upset with me, whether I was deserving of it or not. I could no longer live my life to try to appease him to keep the peace. There was no way to ever reasonably appease him. He would always think what he wanted to think of me, and there was no way I could change his mind, and it was not my battle to fight. I only needed to focus on pleasing God in everything I did. So that night, I wrote up what I thought would be reasonable for a settlement. I no longer cared what Jack would think; I was going to ask for what was fair and let God handle the rest.

God will do as he sees fit.

I did get an apology e-mail from Jack, with text messages with kissing lips and roses attached. I was definitely tired of this roller coaster of back and forth with him. I called my lawyer's office and told his assistant what I agreed to for the settlement. I asked for a higher amount to leave room for negotiation. I was thinking that I would give Jack to come back with a counter offer if he did not agree. I was ready for whatever storm was to follow. I did not hear anything from him right away. When I did, it was not nice. He called me all kinds of names, and blew up my phone with numerous text messages. He claimed that I still loved him and that I want to drag this out for whatever reason. He was clearly delusional. I started to go into my default mode, but I remembered that the blessing always follows the breaking, that it is always darkest before the dawn, that after the storm there is always a rainbow. I was not moved. I had peace with the settlement offer. I had faith that God would do as he saw fit. That night, I prayed and cried out to God, knowing he would hear me and put my mind at ease. He gave me such a sense of calm. I knew he would carry me through this to the end. I knew that worry had no place in my heart since he was with me. I feared no evil because his very same rod and staff protected me. I slept well, and I felt so loved. The power of the Holy Spirit is real, and I was so blessed.

The settlement court date was set up. When we got to court, I was hopeful that we could come to an agreement and be done with it. I got to the courthouse, and Jack was there with his brother. I thought that was strange he was there, but I dismissed it as nothing. My lawyer arrived, and then he went in for a meeting with Jack and his lawyer to see what their counter offer would be. I sat there in the lobby and just meditated on my verses as I did before. I had peace, and I was not worried. After quite some time, my lawyer came out, in a bit of a panic. He said this thing has spiraled completely out of control and has splattered on the floor. He explained that Jack wanted full custody of the girls. He brought his brother so the judge could see who would help him with the girls while he worked nights. My lawyer told me that Jack was claiming that I needed medication, that I was not cooking for the kids, and that the house on Harmony Lane did not have suitable living conditions. I just sat there and listened in complete peace. My lawyer said that if any of this was even remotely true that I had a very big problem. I just looked at him and said none of it was true. He then gave me a piece of paper with the name of the guardian attorney the judge appointed for Chloe and Olivia. He assured me the guardian attorney we were assigned was the best, and she would be able to smell bull crap if it was near her. The paper also listed the amount of money we would each have to pay to cover the attorney fees. He explained that he would also need more money from me if he wanted him to defend me.

I called the guardian attorney immediately and set the appointment for her to meet the girls the following week. I would need four hundred dollars to pay the attorney. I was not worried about that money because I knew God would fight this battle for me. I would also need three thousand to get to my attorney to keep him around. I went back to work after leaving the courthouse. I filled Gina in on all the details. I remember her saying, "How can you be so calm about all this?" It was nothing but God's peace— the peace that passes all understanding, the peace he left with us! His Word was being made real to me. I was not afraid; I was ready for the storm and even more ready for the blessing I knew that was to follow it.

I met with my counselor that day. I let him know what was going on, and he was in utter disbelief. We talked about it, and we prayed. He said something to me that really changed my thinking. He told me that Jack could no longer afford me. At first, I thought he was talking about the amount of money I was asking in the settlement. But no, he meant something more than that. It was priceless to hear that being said to me. I now knew my self-worth and my identity in Christ, and since I really knew it and believed it, I acted like it. Now someone like Jack could no longer afford to have me. He thinks that Jack finally was realizing this, so he had to retaliate by trying to hurt me to regain some sort of control. This was such a revelation, and it unlocked quite a bit for me at the time. I was maturing in my faith, and this was clearly not about me, but God's work in me. The battle for my destiny was still raging, but I knew who already won.

I of course called my mother and my brother to let them know what was going on. I filled in my dad also. They just could not believe that things were going to come down to this. I thought letting everyone around know would give me even more comfort, it did in some ways; but in other ways it did not help. I wanted positive feedback, even though I did not need it. Why was I looking for that in man? The best "nonbeliever" comment I got was, a woman could be a crack addicted whore and a judge will never take kids away from their mother. You have nothing to worry about. Wow, that was comforting! I did turn to God in prayer. He knew my past, and he knew the real fears I had deep down. He knew my failures in the past as a parent. He knew how I was really feeling. I was reminded that there was no condemnation for me. All the scriptures I committed to memory were coming up, and I cried them out loud to God, "You are for me, so who can be against me, Lord? You said there is now no condemnation for those who love Christ Jesus. I love you, Lord. You said no weapon formed against me shall stand. I believe in your promises, Lord. I cast all the anxiety, fear, and guilt at your feet. I will focus on you and not my circumstances. This too shall pass, the victory is already won. In Jesus's name. Amen!"

The days to come were rough in dealing with Jack. He was super cocky now. He just knew that he had the final say in this. He was just awful to me. I would now tape record every encounter I had with him. My brother gave me an old smart phone he had that had a cracked screen. I got the screen repaired and was able to use the phone. Jack would send constant text messages I could now save to the phone. If one of the kids were sick, or if anything went wrong, it was my fault. He would constantly send Bible scriptures trying to condemn me. He mocked my faith and called me a contemporary Christian. He called me self-righteous. He was beating me with the Bible. He was a modern day Judas. I did not stumble. This all made me stronger. It did not matter what he said or thought about me; I knew and believed what God thought about me. I pressed into God even more so now. The more I did, the more comfort, peace, and clarity I would receive.

I took the girls to meet with the guardian attorney. Jack had not made his appointment, so we were able to get in ours before him. She was a really nice woman. She met with me first in her office while the kids waited in the waiting room. She explained she could only talk to the girls without me present. I told her what was going on. I explained Jack's work schedule and our past history. I told her the kids were seeing a counselor, and they were adjusting well. Toward the end of the session, she realized that Jack wanted custody from me. She had thought I was seeking custody from him. She then had a smirk on her face as she realized what was going on. She then said, "Okay, I get it. Let me spend some time with the girls now. She also said that she would have to meet with Jack to listen to his claims, and that he had not made an appointment, but she would be in touch after that. I had explained to the girls that they were going to meet with a woman who needed to let the judge know how they felt about everything that was going on with the divorce. I told them to tell her the truth about how they felt about everything. It was a nice day, so the girls were able to go outside and talk to their lawyer. I was in the lobby, and I could see them talking. They were out there about fifteen minutes. When it was time to leave, the guardian told me she would be in touch. When we got in the car, Chloe commented on how nice the lady was. I asked her if she told the truth when she answered the questions; she said she did. I was glad it was over.

Within the next week or so, I received a packet from my lawyer's office. Inside was the interrogatory questions for me to answer, put together by Jack's attorney. I started to read through them, and my stomach started to churn. There were questions regarding my mental health history, questions about the house we lived in. What the zoning for the house was as well as the square footage. There were also questions asking what actual meals I fixed for the kids. There were questions about my income and retirement. They wanted all my bank statements for the past three years. They wanted all correspondence between Jack and me for the past three years—all e-mails, texts, cards letters, etc. They wanted a list of witnesses who would be willing to testify on my behalf. It was really something. All I could think was, *He really thinks this whole thing is one-sided, and he has done nothing wrong.* This entire thing was a power trip for control. I called my attorney's office and was told to answer the questions and get all the information in as soon as possible. The assistant told me we would draft together questions for Jack to have to answer as well.

When I got home and had the time to really think about all that was going on, it did hit me hard. I leaned into God as I have all along. I looked for a good podcast to listen to. I listened to one from T. D. Jakes. In this one, he was talking about the woman who would go to the temple week after week for years, hoping to be healed from affliction. This one time she gets there, Jesus was actually teaching. T. D. Jakes expressed how the Bible said "He saw her." He made mention that Jesus did not just see her; he saw all of her pain, her struggle, all of it. He saw her. Then Jakes got loud in the teaching and said *"He sees you!"* Jesus sees all you have been through. You do not have to prove anything to anyone. He knows your struggle, and he cares about you, and it is going to be all right." I broke down crying right then and there. I knew it was going to be okay. God was speaking to me through Jakes at that particular moment, and it pierced my heart with a clear revelation: that this was all going to be okay.

At work I let Gina know what all was going on with the interrogatories. She was glad she told me to keep all the e-mails and correspondence over the last year. I let the HR department know the documents I would need. I started on my list of witnesses. There were so many people to include. There were all the people

I worked with at the center who have seen me firsthand with the girls. There was the parent-as-teachers advocate who worked with me and Olivia since she was three months old. There was the inclusion counselor for Chloe who worked with us every year with her special needs. There were all the teachers she had over the years whom Jack had never even met. He had only attended one IEP meeting for Chloe in eight years. There were countless clients who could vouch for my character. Each and every person I contacted said they would testify on my behalf without a problem. These were the blessings from God. He sent his angel armies out once again to rally around me.

I started pulling up old, painful e-mails. It was great that I saved them all. Jack was very good at expressing exactly how he felt; and I had every word of it—pages and pages of it. I had the old voice mails from when I first left him over a year ago. The voice mails clearly showed his violent behavior and angry, abusive language. They also showed his mood swings during that time. The more and more I gathered information, the more confident I became. The only thing I was concerned about was the fact that the house on Harmony was zoned as a one bedroom since the room I was in did not have a door. I talked to some people I worked with who knew the residential building codes. They knew how many square feet would constitute a bedroom. I asked the landlord about getting the house rezoned if possible. He told me he would put a door on or do whatever he needed to do to help me. I was a good tenant, and I was never late with the rent, so he was happy to help me. Everything else was taken cared of; I just had this small worry about the house. I remember a coworker telling me, "It can be taken care of, *if* it even ever has to come to that." He was right. I was getting ahead of myself. I knew who was in charge, and I knew who would always take care of me. I began a three-day fast for confirmation and direction.

I got a call at the desk from guy who wanted to see about getting an inspection on his rental house. I saw his name on the caller ID, and I knew his voice. It happened to be a friend of my brother's, so I identified myself, and he remembered me. I asked if he had a renter lined up, and he told me he did. This whole conversation got me thinking, and from there, I started trying to do things in my own will. It was really weird. That same day, I got this very sharp pain in my neck that just would not stop. It was like God was saying "Be still." I ignored it. Then I ended up driving by the house after work, since it was not far from where Jack lived. When I drove by it, I saw another house on the same street with a For Rent sign in the window. I wrote down the info for that house. The next day, I asked Dee about the house my brother's friend was renting. She told me it was not a good idea, that he was not such a good landlord, and his properties were not well kept. I let it go, but from there I started asking Sarah to keep her eye out for other houses for rent for about nine hundred dollars, and that I wanted at least three bedrooms. She ended up getting me to look at some other houses in a different area that were too far of a drive. I needed something close. My car was old but paid for, so I did not want to have a long daily commute. I knew that none of it was right.

 I called the number of the one house I saw, and I spoke with the owner. I explained they would need to get an inspection done and passed before they could rent the house out. The owner was very glad I had told him that. I asked how many bedrooms it had, and I was told three with a partly finished basement. I then asked the rent, and I was told thirteen hundred dollars a month, and that was way over my budget. I got off the phone, crushed. I got another pain in my neck again. This time, I paid attention. Okay, God. I will be still. I am done worrying about this; I cannot fix it. You have my back, and I will let you drive.

 This was right about the time of the 2012 presidential election. I was listening on the radio about a twenty-one-day call to fast and pray for the nation. It hit my heart hard too fast. I was already into day 3, could I go twenty-one days? I would pray for the strength to do so. I did a liquid fast. I would eat no solid foods. It is amazing what happens during a time prayer and fasting. We become really weak and much more dependent on God. He is made strong in our weakness. Denying your flesh is a way of completely surrendering to God's will, a way to be humbled, helpless, and dependent. During the time, I fasted some truly amazing things happened. The owner of the house I called that needed the inspection, came into city hall to fill out paperwork. I got to talk to him, and he told me to just come and take a look at the house. He said he lowered the price to eleven hundred dollars. I knew that was still too high, but I would let him know. Later that week, Sarah was the one who did the inspection. She told me how cute the house was and that she told him it was priced to high, and he would think about one thousand dollars. I knew I could only do nine hundred, and that was if the amount of child support I asked for was approved. We still had this custody battle in front of us. I put the house out of my head; I just let it go.

I was well into about day 13 of this twenty-one-day fast. I felt so close to God; I was right in step with his will, and I could just feel it. It was the weekend, and I had the girls. I had talked very little to Jack concerning this whole custody thing. The pickups and drop-offs were pretty uneventful. I was able to tell him via e-mail that his pride would be the death of him. He will spend way more money in trying to take the kids away from me, and having the last say—way more money than I ever asked for in the settlement. It was Saturday evening. I kept getting text messages for Jack; he was saying he needed to talk to me. I ignored the texts; he kept texting me. He said he had to see me. I did not want to see him. He would call and I would not answer, but he would keep calling. I finally answered, and he said he needed to tell me something. I told him he would have to tell me in person because there was no way I could record the conversation on the phone. He laughed, and asked why I would need to record anything. I explained he was all over the place from day to day, so I needed to record everything.

That day, I had agreed to see Jack. He came over that evening. He said that he had been thinking about the comment I made about his pride getting in the way. He said I was right about the amount of money it would cost him to fight this. He told me that he did not want to take the kids away from me. He said that he knew the girls loved me and that I was a good mother. He basically recanted every claim he made against me, and I got it all recorded on my phone. He said that he would call his lawyer on Monday to change the paperwork, and that he would sign whatever settlement I agreed to. I could not believe what I was hearing. I was amazed, but not really. It was like Jack had fallen down and hit his head on something. The way he was talking and acting was so strange to me. After he left, I felt it on my heart to eat. I had made chili for the girls that day. Since I was on day 13 of the fast, I was long past feeling the need to eat, but after he left, I got the urge to have a bowl of chili—so I did. God had moved a mountain out of my path just like that! I dropped to my knees and praised him. He was faithful, and he heard my prayer.

People could not believe it! I told my mom and my brother; they were shocked and amazed. A huge burden was lifted. Within the next week, Jack signed the paperwork and assured me it was returned to my lawyer for my signature. Could this really be it? After all that, was this it? Could I exhale? My prayers now were asking if it was in God's will for the kids and me to stretch a little bit. Was it now time for us to move into a bigger place? I just presented my requests to God. If it was his will, he would show me the house.

Sarah came to the desk at work, and she told me the house was not rented out yet and that I should go and look at it at least. She was saying the owner probably would come down off the rent since no one has really looked at the house. So I did call him and scheduled a time to see the house. I went there, and the moment I stepped into the house, I just knew it was where I was going to live. I was not sure how, but I knew this was the house I would live in. It had three bedrooms and a nice yard for the dog, with a little patio. There was a garage and even a basement. I talked to the owner for quite a while that night. He had come off the price to $950 a month. I was really relieved to hear that; I could do that. I had a signed settlement for the divorce, and the amount I would receive monthly would help to pay that amount. I found out the land lord now lived in the neighborhood in West County where I grew up, that was so strange! He told me I would need to fill out an application for a credit check. I knew that my credit would not be favorable. I explained that to him. He said that was fine; it would just give him a better feel about me. He said he did like me, and that was important—that he had a tenant that he liked. My heart still sank because I did not want my past credit history to steal the joys I was seeking for today. Then I remembered the God I served. If it was his will, it would be his bill. He would make a way out of no way.

I filled out the paperwork for the house and dropped it off. I left it at that. I continued to pray that if it was God's will for me to move, it would happen. I got a call from my brother, and his friend was buying a new house, and he had some new furniture to give away. I told him I would take it. Now we still were living in the 624-square-foot home, but we brought the new furniture and fit it in. There was no room to walk, but I was hopeful it would only be temporary. I had claimed the new house, and I was just waiting on God. Then the next day, Josie at work asked if I wanted a big TV she had. She told me her niece was supposed to come and pick it up and never did. I told her yes, I would take it. We went and got it; now there really was no room in my little place. My mother told me about a woman giving away a full-sized Serta bed. I said, "Yes, I do want that for Chloe's room." We got that from her. I was able to get a washer and dryer for, very cheap. I also got a new patio set someone gave me, and a grill. Things were just being brought to me. I did not even ask anyone; it was just the timing of it all—God's timing. He was showing me to be expectant of the blessing. To act as if it was already done, to walk in the faith that it will be given to me.

I had all these things crammed into our little house on Harmony, and no confirmation on the new house. It was going on three weeks, and I had not heard anything back from the landlord. I knew my test here was patience and to know that God was working, even if it did not feel like it—or I could not see it. One early morning during my quiet time, at about 6 a.m., I called out to God to give me a sign, just anything to let me know something about this house. Within about five minutes, I got a text message on my phone. It was from the landlord. He said he could call me tonight. I dropped to my knees and said, "Thank you, Lord!" That night, he did call me. He was going on and on about how he had been on a deer hunting trip since it was the start of the season. He had said that he had no calls on the house until he met with me, and then all of a sudden, he got over forty voicemails. Since he was out of reception range, he did not call any of them back. He went on to tell me that he shot a thirty-point buck on his trip. I had no idea what that meant, and all this time during the conversation I was thinking, *Are you going to rent to me or not?* But I would feel in my spirit, calm down, wait, and listen. He was telling me that he has waited his entire life for that buck. Apparently, it is a big deal to get one that big. He went on about how he was trying to find a local taxidermist to take care of it, and what a hassle that had been. There I was, on the other end, literally about to burst with anticipation. He then says he had no intention to call back or listen to any of those voicemails, that he is very inclined to rent the house to me. My heart sank as he was talking to me. He then said that he would only do a six-month lease to see how I could handle it, since it was an increase for me in rent. I was so excited when I got off the phone; I fell to my knees and praised God. That was the God Almighty interceding on my behalf. I had to walk by faith and not by sight in that situation. In the natural, it looked like I would never get the house—but with God, all things are possible. There is no way I could have ever predicted that to happen or even see it coming. I knew while I was waiting to hear back, God and his angel armies were working on my behalf. I got to work that day and told everyone! They all seemed to think it was luck, but I knew it was nothing but God showing his infinite mercy and love for me—his daughter.

We were able to move into the new house the first week in December 2012. I was a little nervous about being able to swing all the new bills. This house was larger, and we now had a washer and dryer and a dishwasher and a bathtub and central air-conditioning. I cried out to God and asked him to show me how I was going to pay for this house. I knew it was his will to get me in it, so I knew he would not leave me dry as to being able to afford it. Some weeks prior to when we moved, I got a call from an old client who just had a baby. She wanted to know if I was still training, and if I could come to her house while she was on maternity leave and work with her. I told her I would need to pray about it and call her back. I had not trained anyone in quite a while. I felt in my heart that I needed to do it, and I needed the money to put toward a deposit if I were to get a house. I was reminded by the Holy Spirit that the price I charged her needed to reflect a value to the service I was providing. I called her back a few days later and named my package price for ten sessions, which was higher than I'd charged in the past but still very reasonable. She agreed to the price and wanted to start right away. We did. I went to her home, which was close to work two to three days a week during my lunch hour. On the first time I went over, I went right into this sort of mode. It was like I had never stopped training. I just looked at the equipment she had in her home, and we got started. No preparation—it was just effortless for me. She mentioned that I should go back to training. She said she had a tenant who has his own personal training business, and he was doing really well. I just thought to myself that is just not for me.

Since I post everything to my Facebook page—be it good things that happen or bad—people knew what was going on in my life. I give all glory to God. I post things to show how God works in my life through all my different circumstances. The women at work noticed my post about training an old client. They then approached me about getting the lunch group going again. I gave it some thought, and I knew that I would have to attach some value to it if I was going to be involved with them again. The time I spent with those women was very important to me; I would have to stand up and give the service I render some value. I asked each of them to tell me what they spend going out to lunch last week. They each individually e-mailed me back, telling me it was at least fifty dollars. I knew ahead of time that whatever they spent was what I was going to charge them. I replied with the e-mail that would be what they would pay me. There was one person in the group who saw what I was saying, and she said she would do it. The others thought it was too expensive. It was money they were already spending; it was just a matter of how valuable the service was to them. If your goal is to lose weight and get in great shape, why would you be okay to spend money doing things that take you the opposite direction away from your goal? I knew it came down to matter of heart. Where your heart is, your money will follow. If your mind is set on things of the flesh, and you believe the lies of what people in the world have told you, your behavior will reflect that. A peaceful heart will lead to a healthy body. Only a renewing of the mind can change a person's behavior, and I was God's living proof of that.

I sent an e-mail to all the girls who would possibly be interested, and I told them I would now be charging eight dollars a session per person to do a lunchtime workout. In the past, they had only paid between three and five dollars. This is still much lower than the average. Usually small group personal training sessions start at fifteen dollars a person. I was not sure they realized this. I explained in the e-mail that I was not the same person I was before. I stated that I was in a position to give them more than I ever could. I explained in order to lead people, you have to be in front of them—and I, for a long time, was not that. I had nothing inside me to give them, and they were giving me way more than I was ever giving them. I also decided to try and meet with each of them individually just to talk. I was hoping to help unburden them. I wanted to be able to pray for them and speak life into them. I wanted to be able to keep them out of a defeated mindset and encourage them. They were blessings to me in my time of need, and I wanted to give back to them. I got two responses back at first, and then I tried to reach some of the coworkers I worked with at the center. There were four who wanted to come, so the group was now six.

We moved into the house the first week in December—it was great. The kids were so excited, and so was I. I had planned on having a Christmas party at the house at the end of the month. Jack was impressed with the new house. He genuinely told me he thought it was great. I now lived about two blocks away from him, but that was fine. I figured it was part of God's plan. The divorce paper work was signed off by the judge on 12-12-12. That was very significant to me. After a year and a half of back and forth struggle, that was the date it was signed off on. Life was good for me now—divorce final, and a new house. I began to really wonder what was next. I knew that a good work had begun me, but where was God going to take me next? I was going to church regularly. I had a good Bible study group that was about finding significance of life. It was perfect timing. God had placed a girl in my life, Geneva. I met her in Bible study. I knew it was a divine connection. She was a little overweight, and one day after class, she had mentioned that she was thinking about contacting me in the New Year to help her lose weight. At that time, when she said that I felt a stirring in my spirit, it was the Holy Spirit showing me something. I did not disregard it; I was just going to make note of it and keep going. One of the teachings I listened to about finding your purpose had step by step things to do in order to help the Holy Spirit lead you to it. The process involved going back and looking at all the different jobs I ever had, and which ones seemed to come easier for me than the others. I made my list of all the jobs and discovered I felt most fulfilled helping others. I had a servant's heart. All the jobs I did were helping other people and that always made my heart soar. The teaching also instructed to get affirmation from someone who worked closely with me. I got in touch with my fitness mentor, Angel. She affirmed the fact that I did indeed have a special gift in motivating others in fitness. She went on to say it was just a matter of time for me to really realize it in order for me to reach the full potential of being called to do it.

A GLIMPSE OF HIS PLAN REVEALED TO ME

The day after Christmas 2012 until Jan 1, 2013, I spent time praying and fasting. My prayer was for God to show me what my gifts were and what his purpose and plan was for me. I had been listening to a lot of messages being taught about knowing what your God-given purpose is. I was taught that we are all made to do great things. When we lean into our Creator, he is the one who can give us the direction to lead an abundant life. He wants nothing but the best for his children. I knew this because I had seen what he had done for me thus far. I began to have a thirst to go deeper with God and to totally give up the reigns of my life. I now was on his agenda and schedule. I had no plans; he was going to direct all my paths. The plan he had for me was something way better than I could ever plan. I held on to that, I believed it with all of my heart.

During the fast, it was put heavy on my heart to start working with groups of women again. It came to my mind to use the basement to do it. When I first moved into the house, I only saw the basement as somewhere the kids could get loud and play. It never even crossed my mind to train women in the basement. But see? God had already figured it out. When I went with him with my whole heart, he revealed it to me. He gives us just a little at a time because he values the relationship with us; he wants us to come to him every day for all our needs—and I knew this. I walked and talked with God every day. I asked him to reveal a business name for me. During my quiet time, which in the evening time is in that bathtub, he revealed whole peace to me. Whole peace was something he brought me all this way to find. Then I started seeing the logo in my head. The "piece" I was always missing was the knowledge and belief in the love of God, the love I spent all of my life looking for. God dropped this on me, and I just knew I had to do it. Everything started falling into place just that quickly. I remembered Joyce Meyer saying when the Holy Spirit puts something on your heart to do, you either do it, or you feel like you will die if you don't. That was exactly how I felt.

    I talked to my brother about it. He was so excited for me that he gave me a woman's e-mail info that could do my logo. I sent her a paragraph description of what I wanted. She got back to me within two days. I was blown away! She nailed the logo on the first attempt. A girl I had never met or talked to was able to read into the description that was put on my heart. I know this was a blessing from God, and I fell to my knees and thanked him! My brother was very excited; he told me to write everything down. He told me to set up times that I could have people and to pray over them. He told me, in time, the sessions would be filled up. I called a friend from my church Bible study, Geneva. She was someone who had mentioned wanting to work with a trainer in the new year to lose weight. When she had said this a while back, it did spark a stirring in my spirit. I told her all about the logo, and I texted it to her. She was really excited for me and told me to sign her up. So then it began. I posted on Facebook what all was going on, and sure enough, I received many inquiries about group sessions. I had designated Mondays and Thursday to do groups of six. My brother worked with me on my business plan. He kept telling me I would need to offer more times. I was very reluctant at first. I did not want to put so many hours into it. I remembered the past when I would work way too many hours with nothing inside to give, and how that felt. What I began to realize was that it was different this time. I would go work eight hours at city hall, and then run home to what I loved doing. Training with the women was liberating—my heart rate would increase, I would smile, it was effortless. I loved what I was doing. God made me to do this, and I knew it with every fiber of my being.

I had planned out the workout times. It worked great since Jack lived less than two blocks away from the house. That was God's provision. I would need to get the kids at 6 p.m. I got off work at city hall at five. My first session started at 5:15 p.m. I lived very close to work, so everything fell perfectly into place. The kids would come home at 6 p.m. and eat dinner, then I would have a second group 6:30 p.m. until 7:15 p.m. I vowed to never work past 7:30 p.m. I wanted to make sure I had time to spend with the kids. I did not work past six on Wednesday nights, and I was off on Fridays and Sundays.

The basement was nothing special. It just had a concrete floor, plain white walls, and no tiles in the ceiling. I went to the store and bought some weights and some other odds and ends to use. I did not have any real equipment. I did not despise my small beginning. I knew that once God began a good work, he would see it all the way to completion. God provided me with what I would need. None of that seemed to matter to these women. They were drawn in to the light in me. I gave them a great workout; they were there for that and nothing else. My brother had the idea that the women should write their goals on the walls of the basement. During the workouts, I would randomly read something someone wrote on the wall. Their goals written on a place that was anointed with God's love, and me being used as a vessel to help bring things to pass. It was a beautiful thing. Before long, the small groups of six grew to eight, then to twelve, and then to fourteen. Since my job at the desk at city hall, my multitasking skills were sharpened. This came in very handy for working with a group of women all at the same time. I would have to keep my eye on every one of them, and motivate and encourage them throughout the workout. I did add hours to my schedule. I ended up doing nine group session times, and each one God ended up filling within four months' time. My brother would tell me, "You are going to fill up these blank time slots." I had a big, dry whiteboard in my kitchen with the names of all the clients and the session times they would come. He was right—it filled up.

I continued to go to my Father and asked him to equip me to run this race He set before me, and he did. I used to always be in bed before 8:30 p.m., and now I was able to stay up until about ten and be up by 5 a.m. every morning for my quiet time. Things were changing in my life, and I was beginning to live my dreams. My prayer was also that God would bring me the right kind of clients. He did that as well. Many of them would say that I was a blessing for them, and the timing was perfect in their lives to start this journey. I had been thanked for being obedient to my calling. The entire business was ordained and anointed by God. He did it all. The people he sent me were receptive for change and to the things I had to say to them. I spoke life and hope into each and every one of them. My heart was so full of love to give to these women, it would just overflow. I would hug them when they got to my home, and then hug them again when they left. They were my blessings, each and every one of them. I spent time every week on the phone with them. I would talk to them about whatever was burdening their heart. I would take prayer requests. I knew that, as a believer, I could intercede on their behalf to the Father. This was powerful stuff. These women were seeing real change in their lives. Others around them could see it, and they would want to come also. God was overwhelming me every day with these women. This was all because of his love for me. I surrendered to his will, and he was making a way for me. He was making beauty of all my ashes.

There were times before this when I would want to have a mate. I wanted to have someone to share this experience with.

My mind would wander off down that old road, but I realized God knew the petitions of my heart, and he would bring that to pass when the time was right. I knew that I could not get in the mix and try to do things myself. I had wondered about online dating and posted about it on FB. A good Christian friend of mine told me that I needed to listen to God and not take matters into my hands. She was exactly right. God had plans for me, and he was all I needed. He was showing me that all my dependence needed to always be on him. Once I really locked into this, I felt even more peace. On the weekends I would not have the kids, I spent alone with God. It was so awesome to be in his presence. I'd clean the house he provided for me, singing his praises. I'd just marvel at all the food he provided in the refrigerator. I'd plan the workout for the women with such ease and joy. I'd sweep and mop the basement floor with such joy and delight in my heart. It was amazing!

Meanwhile at city hall, things had lightened up tremendously. Gina took another position in another department. They hired an intern to take her place. Her name was Aubrey. She was a very delightful girl. She was very smart, beautiful, and had a wonderful disposition. She was like a breath of fresh air to be around. She was always positive and was always smiling. Thank you, Lord. He knew that with all I was doing, I needed a no-stress level at my daytime job. He provided that in her. I would tell Aubrey all of my business ideas. She was very savvy about all kinds of business aspects. She was very helpful in all the planning stages in my business. She was right there from the very start. God brought her as a helper. I'd bring ideas to her, and she would see different angles that I would miss. She was a true angel.

The workout group at work dwindled down to two people. The clients I had from the center now saw me as competition somehow. I did not see it like that at the time. I was happy to help anyone reach their goals. I would go over and have one-on-one sit down sessions with my old coworker clients I had from there. I was really hurt when they decided it would not be good idea for me to be their trainer. This was spiritual warfare, and I knew how it went. I told Satan he had no dominion in my life or my thoughts. I was a new creation, and he would not make me feel defeated or rejected. I knew God had other plans for me. That was tremendous growth for me. I was no longer a victim of my circumstances. My mother would chime in from time to time with her seeds of doubt. She would tell me I was doing too much. I told her that I was being obedient to my calling, and I felt more alive than I ever have. I had been given a life of purpose. I told her that God was equipping me to run this race for him. She decided to come and try one of my sessions. She had figured out which two days a week she would come. When it came time for the class, she cancelled the day before. I could not worry about her. Just like with all my clients, the timing had to be right for them in order for anything to happen. I could meet them half way, but they have to be receptive to starting.

The kids loved the women coming in and out of the house. They knew I was doing something I loved, and they loved to hear me "boss the ladies around." Eventually, Jack agreed to drop the kids off at the house at 6 p.m. This would make things easier for me. He was now dating someone, so he would go and meet with his new woman after he dropped the kids off. He would then see all the women leaving the house. From time to time, he would make snide remarks, but I paid him no mind. I was doing God's will in my life, and I could not be happier. He had started dating, and he made it my business to let me know all the details. He said he would want the same courtesy. I did not see it as a courtesy, as I really did not care what he was doing. I was just praying for him to change his ways, for God to continue to soften his heart.

I planned to do a boot camp. Aubrey had helped me with the details of it. I found a central location that would charge a reasonable rental fee. My goal was to have at least twenty-five people. I put quite a bit of focus into this. I got the insurance I needed to have, and everything was a go. The only problem was that no one was signing up. I had about five people interested. I had flyers given out at Olivia's school. Chloe's teacher sent a mass e-mail to the entire teacher list in the school district. Still, there was little response. I thought, *Okay, God, I prayed about this. If it is not your will, that is okay. Show me what it is you'll have me do.* Then a client from church came to me with this wellness initiative they were trying to start at her job. She was telling me the opportunity in corporate fitness was needed. My focus now was to get out of my full-time job. Just maybe God's plan was for me to do something like this. I thought if I could get some corporate contracts, I could be out of city hall in a matter of months. I began to talk to Audrey about it. She knew all the facts about what companies looked at from an administrative point of view. She was studying this sort of thing in her schooling. She could see the need and how I could be of help. I asked different clients if there was someone in their HR department I could send a proposal to. I sent out a couple. Aubrey had agreed to help me get together a PowerPoint presentation. Somewhere down the road, this all went cold. Apparently, the budgets they had were already in place, so most would need to start something like this the following year, if they were going to do it. The client I had from church dropped the subject and stopped coming to my sessions altogether. It was really strange. I just felt maybe I was doing things out of God's will. I knew that when things were according to his will, they would just flow almost effortlessly.

I had gotten word from Jack that the woman he was dating was now his fiancée, and he was going to get married. This was a complete shock since he had only been dating her for a month or so. I was worried for our girls. I felt like they were being backed into a corner without getting the chance to really know this person. I really thought this was moving way too fast for them. I was right. Olivia started wetting the bed and having stomachaches from the stress of everything. She was used to being the baby, and this woman had a daughter who was younger than her. Now it seemed Olivia was demanding more attention from me and during the workout time I had with my clients, she would do everything she could to disrupt it. Chloe was having angry outbursts at school that her teacher was concerned about. I knew that this was spiritual warfare again. I prayed for my kids and for this new woman Jack had met. This was spiritual warfare, which meant there was a blessing right around the corner for me. That was always the way it went. I knew that after the trial was always the blessing. After the storm was always a rainbow. I knew to trust God through all things, and he would bring it all together for my good. He did just that.

I began to pray and fast again for direction and comfort during this transition with the girls. It was put heavily on my heart at this time to write my story. I had this urge to compile all my journals over the years to write a book. I had no idea how to do it, or why I was supposed to, but I knew it was something God wanted me to do. I was given that same conviction as I did starting the business. I did some research online, and Tate Publishing literally popped up on my screen. I read the information, and then sent an e-mail in to get more information. I received the information and did not really do anything with it. I saw that they only publish 4 percent of the work they received, so I felt like there was no way. I had no writing skills; I did not even finish community college. I momentarily forgot who was in charge. It was not about what I could or couldn't do, but about what his will would be for me. Later that week, I sent an e-mail to the acquisitions editor. I explained how my life had dramatically changed since I gave Christ the reins. She told me it sounded great and that I should get some chapters together for a manuscript to submit. I thought about it.

Then we got a massive snowstorm in our area in April 2013! It was the weekend of Palm Sunday—and we had snow? The kids were with their dad, and I was snowed in. I had this huge urge to start writing, so I did. I sat down on a Saturday and kept writing until almost 2 a.m. that night. That Sunday was Palm Sunday, and the snow really picked up. I stayed home from church and continued writing this manuscript. The words were just pouring out. It was nothing but the power of the Holy Spirit working in me. I finished things off and sent the manuscript in an e-mail to the editor. I got an e-mail back that day—Palm Sunday. It was not an auto-generated e-mail either. I was told that she liked what I wrote, and I would be hearing from her soon. I was shaking with excitement. I was obedient to the Holy Spirit. I did not know what would come of it, but it was put in my heart to do, so I just did it, no questions asked. I shared what I sent in with Geneva, my client, from church. She loved what she read! It actually unlocked some things she was dealing with. She said that my honesty about my broken past helped her in a way she could not describe. We talked for over an hour on the phone. She was in tears. I was moved. I realized right then my story could help someone else. This was a huge revelation, and I felt so compelled to act even more now. I sent the manuscript to a few other clients, and the responses were overwhelming. I thought if I did not get a book deal, it was enough to know I could impact people with my story. I had another client tell me she did not know I wanted to write a book; I told her I didn't either. She told me her father had written a couple of books, and she brought one to me. The book was about how to pray. It was a book published by the same publishing company I just submitted the manuscript to. I was floored.

I was seeing what God was showing me. It was his will. I was not even worried. That next week, I got the e-mail from Tate that had the in the subject line: "Tate loves your work!" I was shaking when I opened the e-mail. There was a contract attached. They wanted to write my story! I fell to the floor and thanked God. I knew it was his will. I had to pay a refundable deposit to show that I was committed. I happened to have the funds in the bank since I was saving for a car. My plan was to save for a car, but God's plan was obviously something better than that. I did not hesitate in using the savings for his purpose.

The week I was to sign the contract, adversity came my way from all sources. This was all expected because the closer I get to where God was taking me, the forces of darkness try to pull me right back down where I came from. I understood this all too well. That week, there was a thunderstorm that knocked the power out while we were at church. We went home, and since I enter the house through the garage with the garage door opener, we were locked out of the house because there was no power. The girls were hungry, and I was not sure where we were going to go. My brother did not have power at his house either. I took he kids to a pizzeria that did have power. After that, we went to stay at a hotel. I was flustered because it was a school night, and we did not have anything with us, and I was not sure what the plan was. We get into the room and Olivia, my five-year-old took time out to investigate the room. She found the Bible in the drawer and said, "There is a Bible here, Mama. We need to calm down and read it." She was exactly right. I ran over to her and hugged and kissed her. This was a reminder I needed at that exact moment. We made it through that night. I called the neighbor the next morning to see if the power was restored—she said it was. We had breakfast, and then made it home to change and get to school. Later that day, I received an e-mail that made me upset. I had sent the manuscript to someone who was a past client whom I felt was a good friend who cared about me. The e-mail was attacking me, saying that I may have some unresolved bitterness and unforgiveness issues that I need to take care of, and writing a book is not the way to do it. I was taken off guard, but I knew what I was dealing with. That same night, Olivia came into my bed at night, wet it, and then she would get up and go back to her bed. Then the next night, Olivia cut her ponytail off before bed. I did not discover it until the morning. So we had to get her to the hair place to cut it all down even. I was late to work, and she was late to school. This was all days before I was to sign the contract. I signed the contract anyway. God's will for my life prevailed. Once I did that, I felt fabulous!

I was on top of the world, and I wanted everyone to know it. I made the mistake of thinking everyone would be as excited as I was. No! That was not the case. Not everyone who smiles in your face is not with you. I soon could tell who was a supporter and who was not. All my clients were supportive and excited for me, but the haters mostly remained either skeptical—and the worst, silent. The people at work withdrew from me really fast. I was being taught something. I paid attention to what God was showing me. I learned to become humbled and kept my plans to myself. This was something I prayed about, and little by little, I was able to contain my joy. If a client or an interested person would ask, I would gladly talk about how God was clearly working all things together for my good. I now began to work hard on getting the book finished. I would write every day and on the weekends. When the girls were with their father, I would take the entire weekend and write. I soon learned writing the book was a process God was taking me through. I was able to recall different times in my life where he was always there, waiting for me to reach out to him. I had uncovered memories of how I was raised, and I went through life without any idea of who I was. What I clearly was beginning to see was that God had big plans for me, and I had to get out of my own way to let his will be done.

My son Blake called me, and he was telling me about a woman he met on the train. He told me that she spoke prophecy to him. She told him God put it in her heart to tell him that he can do what it is he wants to do with God's help. My son told me this was the conviction he needed to give his life to the Lord. He has seen what God was doing in my life, and he had many experiences that he knew were beyond him. I had been praying in my confessions that all my children would grow up to lead Christian lives. My oldest son had come to Christ; I could not be happier. On the following Sunday, he drove home and came to church with me. My heart was so full.

> As for me and my house, we shall serve the Lord.
>
> Joshua 24:15 (NIV)

I continued to walk with God daily for direction. I steadily would continue to see how the lives of my clients would change. More and more, clients were being added. I got a notice of a garnishment that would be put on my paycheck. When I got the news, I did not even freak out because I knew my father in heaven had it covered. Every time something came at me, there was always a blessing right behind it. I got the garnishment, and at that same time, God brought thirteen new clients. I was clearly being taken care of by my Father. I was now at full capacity with doing business out of my basement. My clients had been mentioning my looking at space to rent a few weeks prior. I remember telling them, "No, we are fine in the basement." I did not even realize where all of this was going. One had the idea of renting space from the high school or even the park. I dismissed it all. My one client told me she saw some space over by the Dollar General. I thought nothing of it.

I had a dentist appointment, and as I was leaving the dental office, no one would let me make a left hand turn. I sat there for over five minutes, and then I decided to just turn right with the flow of traffic to see if I could find another way home. I drove and kept driving until I could tell where I was. I noticed I was coming a different way, but I was coming up on the intersection where the Dollar General was. I knew there was a reason I was there, so I turned into the lot and just looked at the spaces available. I could not find a pen in the car, so I committed the number to memory. I got home, and I went about my business, but something kept nagging at me to call the number, so I did. There was a man who picked up the phone. I rambled on about how I thought I was looking for space because my home-based business has outgrown my house. I told him I knew nothing about the process or what something like that cost. I told him I worked at city hall, so I was familiar with the different applications. He then asked me if I was the black woman who was always so efficient and polite at the front desk. *Yes!* That was me. *Whatever your hands find it to do, do it to glorify the Lord.* He knew who I was. He told me the space was a thousand square feet, and the rent was much less than I ever imagined. He told me they just went through the entire process of getting the area zoned for fitness and dance. He told me there would be a dance studio next door. I asked if there was a deposit. He said there was none. He said we would need to decide on flooring, and I could be in the space in as soon as three weeks. I was overwhelmed, and I told him I would have to think about it and call him back. I hung up and fell to my knees once again! I was in utter disbelief, but at the same time, I knew my God was awesome!

During the next night, I had some new clients show up, and I had mentioned that we were looking to move into a space. I found out the new client who loved the workout was friends with the owner of the dance studio I would be next door to. God is just making a way everywhere I turn. His love is real—and it is good, it is faithful, it will never fail. I will live my life looking to him to show me what to do. He has a plan for each and every one of us, and it is my prayer for everyone to get to know him for who he is, and let him direct them into the destiny he has for them.

I am near the completion of writing this book. In less than a month, I will be moving into a commercial space for my business. Everything is going very smoothly because of God's grace.

I got a reasonable bid for the flooring, which the landlord will pay, and I was given the first month rent-free. My clients have given all kinds of suggestions and ideas for the new space. They were all excited and so supportive of me. At the same time as all of this is happening, my job at city hall has taken a drastic turn. They implemented a new software system, so essentially I had to relearn everything. The stress level is high all around because there are quite a few problems with the system, and no one really knew what they were doing. I had peace that surpassed all of this. God also took away more people were around me who were causing me harm. I'd just smile and know that I am loved and that this is all very temporary. There were so many people who willingly helped me when I was down at the beginning of this journey—now they were very distant. Once God began to rule my life and I was made new, these very same people one by one became silent and withdrew from me. I did nothing to deserve this. But then I remember Jesus was despised and rejected, and since he lives in me, I will also share in this suffering. This was a painful reality that God has shown me, but it is a lesson I will always remember.

The pressure continued to build when I received an e-mail from my boss saying that I would need to submit a formal request to pursue my business and remain a full-time employee. I was shocked since I had this business with all the proper business license paperwork from the city since January. I went ahead and typed up a quick letter, signed it, and went to scan it in—and the scanner would not work. I asked Aubrey my coworker to try it, and she could not get it to work from her computer either. We had another person who helped install the scanner try, and he could not get it to work either. Okay, God, I get it. I am not to submit the letter. So I did not. I went home that night and prayed and fasted the next couple of days to get in alignment with what God wanted me to do. I asked for revelation and clarity and for him to show me the way I needed to go. He definitely made it clear. All the negative things about the workplace all of a sudden came to mind, with the garnishment—the new software, the attitudes of people, and then the request for permission to run my business. God was making it uncomfortable for me at that job, so I would move to the next level. I realized Satan would keep me comfortable in mediocrity sometimes so I would not reach out to do what God needed me to do. All these things were telling me it was time to move. Then I went for a run that morning with my dog and out of nowhere, a deer came out up ahead of us. She sort of hung around and did not really scamper off too quickly. My dog wanted a closer look, but she remained calm. I was trying to process what we should do. We continued on our path, and the deer made its way back into the woods. Then the Holy Spirit settled it into my heart. The deer! I remembered my circumstance before I was able to move into the house I was now living in. On paper, it did not look like I would get the house. Looking at my finances, it did not look like I could afford it either. But through a deer, God made a way for me, and that is what he was showing me at that very moment. My prayer for revelation and conviction about leaving my job at city hall and pressing forward to the goal that God had for me was made just like that! I got home and took a shower. I had the radio on, and the words of the song played speaking about walking by faith. It was evident that I was to step out on faith and trust in the Lord, who had never failed me since I answered his call. I went in that day, typed up my letter of resignation, signed it, and it scanned without a problem!

Once the decision was made for me to resign, everything with the business preparation fell right into place. I signed the lease. I was shocked at low cost of health insurance for myself. The liability coverage payment was deferred for thirty days, and even then I'd needed only to pay 40 percent. I got an ad placed for my open house without seeing a proof or even paying for it as I had called it in on the deadline day. The ad printed perfectly. The chamber of commerce waived a fee for me, and planned my ribbon cutting for the day of my open house. God expanded my vision and sent four great employees to train. These women came to me with the same passion to help people. God has equipped me with a team. He has made it so obvious to keep moving forward and not look back—that he has made a way for me, I only need to continue to seek him and obey.

I submitted my resignation letter on June 6, 2013. I realize I was molded by all my experiences as an employee at city hall. It was my training ground. I was brought up and matured to be able to complete the calling God has placed on my life. I am saddened that many others around me do not understand that. Some took the news of my leaving and personalized it. They tried to invoke fear into my decision, the same fear that they themselves feed off of. That is what keeps them in the same place they are for years, trapped in mediocrity, right where Satan wants them to live. To them I say this: Jesus died so we could have life to the fullest, and fear is a lie. We are to fight fear with faith and step out of Satan's plan and look to what God's plan is for us. I pray you see God for all he really is in my story, and know that you can have your own story as it is a free gift. The only question is, will you accept it?

AFTERWORD

We opened Whole Peace Fitness on June 29, 2013. This was part of God's plan for me. I trusted in him the entire way, and he met me with every step I took. He brought the space, the staff, and he provided the funds to meet the needs. I did not take a business loan to open the location. The grand opening was more incredible than I can ever describe. I was shocked and awed. There were over 150 people there, and I could feel God's presence and his smile over me the entire day. All my children were there, as well as my mother and my brother. The most amazing unexpected thing happened that day, a friend of mine from high school that I had not seen in years showed up to the grand opening. She handed me a bouquet of flowers, the flowers really stood out to me because there was a giant sunflower in the bouquet. At that particular moment I knew that my grandpa Jones was very proud of me as well. Four days after the opening on July 3, 2013, was my last day at city hall. I left quietly without a fuss, and that is exactly how I wanted. The quiet ending is only the beginning of something more spectacular than I will know at this point. I am so thankful that I have arrived at Whole Peace in my life. It is the peace of God that was freely given to me as a gift, and now I can walk throughout the rest of my life and into eternity with this fantastically wonderful gift.

Grand Opening Whole Peace Fitness June 2013

The Power of Prayer
I want to add that I truly believe in the power of prayer. Throughout my life I am sure many people including my mother prayed for me to change my ways and stop repeating my mistakes. The times my family seemed distant I believe they were still praying for me. My mother I know prayed for me. She may not have had all the right answers in dealing with me but she got it right with asking God to help where she fell short. The Holy Spirit will fill in where we cannot. I have not been the perfect parent to my kids but I pray for them daily. The Holy Spirit will take care of the rest. I cannot help but look at the words my mother wrote on the Bible she gave to me in 2004.

To Casondra,
 May you use this Bible forever. I love you and I am proud to be your mother.
Mom. April 2004
 I never even opened or started reading this Bible till late 2010. This shows me that she was doing all she could to show me a better way to live and I just did not receive it until I was ready to. Now, I read that very same Bible everyday and in fact all of the verses quoted in this book are highlighted straight from that very Bible my mother gave me over 10 years ago

TESTIMONIALS

I have known Cassie for almost 15 years. We started working together at an all women's fitness facility. We lost touch after it was sold and we went out different ways.

One day I decided that I was going to start looking for a personal trainer. I started asking around but nothing totally felt right, or was within my price range. I happened to be scrolling through my news feed on Facebook one day and there it was, the post from Cassie that she had started personal training out of her home, and it was perfect for my price range! Talk about meant to be! It has been one of the best moves I have ever made!

Since training with Cassie I feel the best I have in years. Not only physically but she also spiritually guides us.

At Whole Peace Fitness we are truly a family. All the clients work together to help each other achieve their goals. We motivate each other, we pick each other up when down, we congratulate each other on their achievements.

I have met a whole new group of AWESOME women and it's all in thanks to Cassie.

Cassie, you are the best, and we all love you to the moon and back!

—Kathy Springmeyer

I was led to Cassie's basement by an old friend from high school whom I'd recently re-connected with. From the moment I showed up and worked to catch up to the group (I'm always late for everything), Cassie was welcoming and I could already tell she was not going to be an "average" trainer. There was more depth to what she wanted us to take away from our time with her. What she challenged us to do was to think differently. She told us we CAN do anything we put our mind to and that it all starts with what you believe about yourself. Cassie really did want us to be our best selves; not just on the outside, but she wanted us to be the best we could be on the inside too! She is a very inspiring woman and her emotional strength never ceases to amaze me.

—HM

August of 2013 started a new chapter in my life with you and Whole Peace Fitness. I was a "couch potato", and now I am working out 3 days a week. You have helped me to become stronger and healthier. I am more self-confident than I have ever been in my life. I owe that to you. You are a great trainer and a very inspirational person. I have a whole new outlook on life – I can do this instead of I can't do this! Thank you!

—Tricia Belter
Bridgeton, MO

I met Cassie Booth back in August 2013. I met her at a woman's networking group one afternoon. She gave away a free 6 session punch card to her gym. I was the lucky winner that day! I started at Whole Peace Fitness August 12, 2013. From that day, it has changed my life dramatically. Once I started working out and feeling amazing from the inside out my life started becoming whole! Cassie has gone above and beyond what any trainer/gym owner has ever done. She loves and cares for each individual who steps into her facility. As the months went on, Cassie and I have become incredible friends. She has helped me out spiritually, mentally, physically and emotionally. Cassie puts her whole heart into her career and into her gym. Cassie is a very spiritual woman and it shows in everything that she does. Whole Peace fitness is Faith based and the woman there all have something in common, some way, some how. Her book *Journey to Whole Peace* hit personally as a woman. I read the book after I had been going to the gym and it has opened my eyes to see the importance of the gym, the reason why it began, and the reasoning why it is here. The book is about a woman who has struggled in life and now has turned her life over to GOD. There is a reason we all live the life we have. We all have a plan. Cassie's plan is forming all around her and around her facility. Whole Peace Fitness and *Journey to Whole Peace* will touch so many woman. It's says that we, as woman can do whatever we put our minds too. Congratulations to my best friend Cassie Booth. You have done amazing work for the world as a whole and in me as well. I wish you great success in life and will be here with you every step of the way!

—Heather McAdams
Troy, MO.